BRIGHT YOUNG THINGS

LONDON

© 2002 Assouline Publishing, Inc.
Photographs © 2002 Jonathan Becker

Assouline Publishing, Inc.
601 West 26th Street
18th floor
New York, NY 10001
USA
Tel.: 212 989-6810   Fax: 212 647-0005

www.assouline.com

ISBN: 2 84323 337 2

Color separation: Gravor (Switzerland)
Printing: Amilcare Pizzi (Italy)

Copyedited by Margaret Burnham

Brooke de Ocampo

BRIGHT YOUNG THINGS LONDON

Photographs by Jonathan Becker

ASSOULINE

For Emilio, Inès, Isabel and Marina,
the source of my energy, inspiration and happiness.

CONTENTS

FOREWORD

BY FLEUR COWLES

The future belongs to the young. This thought gives me pleasure and impatience, as I've made it part of my life to know and to judge the youth of my time.

I was inspired to do this when I discovered that Brooke de Ocampo (who brought me the invitation to write this foreword) told me how much she enjoyed reading my book *Tiger Flower* when it was published many years ago, and is currently reading it to her little daughters.

Since I have always had a passionate interest in the young, I was pleased and eager to cooperate. Apart from all else, I am proud to be a part of a beautiful and imaginative publishing event.

I, too, was very young when I published the very first issue of *Flair* magazine in 1950, which had to survive a combined attack from all other competitive class magazines.

Fortunately, the new Bright Young Things will have neither enemy, jealousy nor envy to overcome.

Looking back fifty years, I admire and perhaps envy the bright young women of today. They are better educated and have thrown off the shackles of inhibition and earned complete freedom of choice. Marriage has become an option, not a necessity, and any position in our western society is open to them, provided they have the talent and ability and are prepared to make the sacrifices of high office in whatever sphere it demands.

The communists eventually discovered that there was no substitute for the embrace of family, especially in times of crisis and grief. I think the bright young men and women of today—provided they combine the best of the old with the best of the new—should live a happier and more fulfilled life.

INTRODUCTION

BY NICHOLAS COLERIDGE

One blustery New York afternoon in Autumn of 2000, I wandered into the Madison Avenue Bookshop and was confronted by a huge display of a new book called *Bright Young Things*. It wore a scarlet jacket with gloriously clashing orange endpapers that compelled you to pick it up. Inside were dozens of portraits of sleek, smart, young New Yorkers, posing in their uptown apartments and downtown lofts or on the wide terraces of art-filled penthouses. Most, though not all, of these happy-looking singles and couples bore branded surnames such as Rockefeller, Herrera, Loeb, von Furstenberg, Lauder, Hearst and Lauren.

I bought a copy and read it in the back of a yellow cab on the way to JFK, then I read it some more on my flight home to London. It was impossible not to feel slightly intimidated by the beautiful, well-groomed people on display. Their lives, so far as one could tell, had achieved the highest levels of per-fection and personal karma. Their apartments were decorated with originality and flair. On their walls hung striking paintings by Cy Twombly, Jasper Johns and Jean-Michel Basquiat. As if that wasn't already annoying enough, they appeared to work rather hard too, and to be conspicuously successful in their various careers, and to be married to other handsome, successful people. There were no two ways about it: the impeccable investment bankers, interior designers, glossy magazine journalists, cosmetics and fashion heiresses and MTV presenters who filled the pages of *Bright Young Things* inhabited an enviably golden American universe.

Of one thing I was quite certain: it would be impossible to recreate such a book in Britain. People like that didn't exist in London. As a capital, we could never hope to aspire to that level of perfection. We pay insufficient attention to personal grooming, our dentists let us down, and the young don't have modern art collections to compare with those of Manhattan. The British, I reflected, are a nation of makers-do. We live surrounded by hand-me-down furniture, in old houses and blocks of flats, cutting corners and making the best of things. For financial and cultural considerations too complex to analyze fully in this introduction, our homes are altogether shabbier, scruffier, more eccentric and rougher-round-the-edges. How could anyone hope to find thirty movers and shakers in London to equal the taste brokers of Manhattan?

Eighteen months later, I was invited out of the blue to lunch at Harry's Bar by Brooke de Ocampo, whom I recognized as the author of *Bright Young Things*. She preferred not to elaborate on the motive behind the lunch, saying only that there was "something she wanted to run by me." I had read enough about Brooke in glossy British magazines to know that she had recently relocated to London with her

Argentinean husband, Emilio, and their three young children. Having worked for American *Vogue*, *Harper's Bazaar* and Sotheby's in New York, she had a reputation for being bright, energetic and beautifully dressed. I wondered what it was that she wanted to ask me.

Over lunch, she explained that she was well advanced in editing a British edition of *Bright Young Things*. Most of the pictures had, in fact, already been taken by the same acclaimed *Vanity Fair* photographer, Jonathan Becker, who had worked on the New York edition.

I was astonished. "But you've only just arrived in London. How have you found all the people?"

She reeled off a long list. It was pretty well faultless, spanning at least five of the overlapping circles that comprise London's social and artistic tribes. There was no question but that she had done her homework. The London book, like its predecessor, embraced interior decorators (as we call them over here), fashion entrepreneurs, flavor-of-the-moment architects, supermodels and stylists, champion socialites and artists. In a city as private and, some say, socially impenetrable as London, Brooke de Ocampo had managed, in less than six months, to coax half of the most interesting inhabitants into her book. The scope was impressive too—from Chester Square to Hoxton Square and back again. By the end of lunch, I had gladly agreed to write the introduction to Brooke's book about the city in which I was born and raised, and where I have spent my whole adult life.

Perhaps it takes an outsider's eye to successfully identify a cast of characters like these. Looking through the photographs, I realize how current the choice is. There is something definitely modern about the group Brooke has put together. She has avoided all the English clichés: there are no dusty aristocrats here, no red-faced young squires, no "it" girls, few blatant self-publicists, no sad "identikit Sloanes," tabloid soap stars, pop princesses or minor royals. Instead, we are presented with cool urban achievers and overachievers, entrepreneurs and wild style frontiersmen.

I am struggling to get through this introduction without using the word "eclectic" more than half a dozen times, but eclectic is the adjective that keeps pushing to the fore. The Londoners in this book have amassed eclectic collections of nineteenth- and twentieth-century paintings, Afghan rugs, limited edition art and fashion photographs, lead soldiers, busts of Lenin, knickknacks and—let's admit it—junk. There are fewer museum-quality pictures by contemporary artists than in the New York volume, but the eye for beauty is no less keen. The colors on the walls of London homes and in the choice of fabrics are frequently bolder, too, and there is a greater tolerance for the unusual and quirky. Probably I am hopelessly biased, but I think Londoners demonstrate more wit and personality, and a greater willingness to break the rules, than their transatlantic counterparts.

Since this selection of Londoners is itself eclectic, it is impossible to generalize. The only things, stylistically, that they have in common is a taste for zebra skins and tiger rugs, pillars—these pillars of modern society—and framed photographs of their friends and small dogs. I counted nine real little dogs in the book before losing score. There are lots of pairs of shoes, too, which has always been a London thing. The only other characteristic many of this group share is a fondness for eating lunch at George, Mark Birley's chic new club in Mount Street, so it seems appropriate that George's chef, Daniel de la Falaise, features as a pivotal Londoner in the mix. But, as I have said, you cannot generalize: the dramatis personae are culled from the discordant worlds of *Wallpaper* to *Dazed & Confused* by way of *Vogue, Tatler* and *Vanity Fair*. It is like the best kind of party, at which half the guests are old friends and the other half like each other on sight.

The players on these pages are by no means all lifelong Londoners; many have only lived here for a few years. They have migrated to the city to work in banking or fashion, part of the financial and cultural diaspora that has established London as the world's most international capital. This book reflects the tastes of a particular new species of Londoner: widely traveled, cosmopolitan, open to new influences and ideas. I estimate that two-thirds of the people in this book each take more than fifty flights a year. They are almost as familiar with the sidewalks of New York and Tokyo—as well as the ski lifts of Aspen, the temples of Cambodia and the beach bars of St. Barts—as they are with the garden squares and cobbled mews of London. One reason they and their houses are so interesting . . . so eclectic . . . is because they are forever making new, surprising discoveries on their travels. They have the where-withal and the courage to mix things up.

For the most part ferociously well-organized, their lives and houses resonate with effortless ease. Of course, as we all know, nothing requires more effort than the illusion of effortlessness, and nothing is so difficult to achieve as an inspiring but relaxed environment. *Bright Young Things* is brimming with the best examples. Who would ever have supposed that London had it in her?

RITA KONIG

BY HONOR FRASER

From Reginald to Elton, from Eldrick to Tiger, from Norma to Marilyn. We have come to know and love many of the brightest things since they underwent name changes. Some people might not know that Rita Konig was once christened "Henrietta." In fact, she was Henrietta until she left school. Many people knew and loved her even then, the goldilocked Heathfield graduate with quite a long name. It was at one of her dinners—she had been throwing them since she was fifteen—that a particularly cheeky relation ventured to refer to his hostess as "Rita." And lovely Rita, who is always dashing about in her silver Beetle and also permanently involved in altercations with meter maids, was, from that moment on, known by everyone as Rita.

With a new short name came a new short hairstyle. Short bobbed blonde was white hot; long golden locks were quite not. Since these two invigorating moments, Rita has not looked back. Dazzling people wherever she goes with her exuberance, her style and her sense of fun, she has made social and professional connections throughout London and across waters to foreign cities in all directions (although I am not sure she has hit Anchorage as yet).

Since the Henrietta days, and until very recently, Rita's work base was running her mother Nina Campbell's shop on Walton Street. From there, she has built up a client list for whom she has done extensive interior decorating work. More importantly however, she has built up invaluable knowledge of who, where and how in the world of contemporary living. If there is anything you need for your home, your dinner party, your wardrobe, your sponge bag, Rita will know the best place to get what you are looking for in London, New York or Los Angeles. It is for this reason that, a year ago, British *Vogue* commissioned Rita to write a monthly column for their lifestyle pages. In the column, Rita offers domestic tips as everyone's domestic darling. The name of the column, of course, is "Rita Says." Her home is always filled with friends and is very much the center of her life. She has every confidence in the great entertaining space that she has created and so is a voracious and successful entertainer. Her profession is a natural extension, in fact, of her seemingly effortless ability to create the stylish and youthful living environment in her own home. It is for this reason that she has recently been commissioned by Ebury Press to write a book about the possibilities for the home in which she will impart, to those of us who are clueless and need help, her unparalleled ability to make the most of how you live. And having known her and considered her a great friend for years, I can assure you this is something she knows all about.

BY NATASHA GARNETT

Rita Konig—designer, columnist, writer, consummate entertainer, raconteuse and sybarite—is a girl with a great many strings to her rather stylish bow. As at home on the grouse moor as she is on the dance floor of a downtown Manhattan club, Rita glides through society and lights up a great many rooms around the

Previous page: Rita Konig in her bath filled with bubbles, wearing her grandfather's top hat. On the walls painted Lido, a color by Nina Campbell at Paint Library, hang the antlers from a stag Rita shot in Scotland.

Above: Black-and-white photos taken with a vintage Polaroid Land camera of friends and holidays are carefully stuck to the kitchen wall. Below: A Venetian gold glass lamp sits on an old mirrored coffee table from David Champion, among a collection of rose-colored glass vases and ashtrays.

Opposite: A silk purple eye mask embroidered with the words "Bad Girl" against pressed linen sheets on Rita's bed. The wallpaper is Madras Violet, by Cole & Son.

Witty, caustic, sexy, generous and, to be honest, quite the noisiest person I have ever met, Rita never fails to beguile, charm and dazzle anyone she meets. She is not so much the center of attention but the center of things.

Sometimes she is the child, brimming with excitement, giggles and enthusiasm, staring at you with those large blue eyes. At others, she is the wise old Duchess proffering advice with that haughty confidence that only she can get away with.

Her greatest love affair in life has been her telephone, which she could not live without, although she has to regularly as she is always losing it. She will talk to a friend in need for hours on end, and if that wasn't enough, once she's hung up, she descends in person with coffee and cakes.

But Rita's greatest gift, other than the fact that she can outtalk anyone I know, is her sense of style. If her flat and her dress sense, weren't testimony enough to this, then it is her recently commissioned book—which even gives tips on how to iron with flair—and her much admired and followed style column in *Vogue*. This is a girl who wasn't born with a silver spoon in her mouth but a swatch book. She has a Midas touch, a sixth sense when it comes to interiors and is the only designer I have ever known who has made a bag of Tate and Lyle Sugar into an objet d'art.

Previous pages, left: An early 20th-century watercolor of Durham Cathedral on the sitting room wall, next to a Lenare photograph of Rita's grandmother. Right: Rita in a spun silk top hat from the early 1900s, originally made for her grandfather, from Herbert Johnson.
Opposite: On Rita's fireplace mantle in her bedroom are photographs by Ellen von Unwerth, her grandmother's travel clock, and bottles of scent. The "H" reflected in the mirror is for Henrietta, Rita's full name.

DAVID ADJAYE

BY EVE MCGREGOR

When my husband, Ewan, and I first met David Adjaye at our St. John's Wood house on a hot June morning in 1997, it was clear to both of us that he was no ordinary architect. Aside from his good looks and his ineffable charm, he had the most amazing childlike passion and enthusiasm about the possibilities of transforming the three flats in front of us into our family home. By the end of our first meeting, we both saw there was no need to look any further. David had literally charmed the keys off us there and then.

After three years of planning, designing and endless discussions on how best to create an ideal living space for my family, we are now living in a functional, stylized house with David's beautiful reinterpreted wall paneling throughout. Through all the requisite ups and downs of such a process, we have also become good friends. And true to David's character of individual care and concern (though he has now moved on to such huge, socially centered commissions as the £25 million Idea Stores for the London Borough of Tower Hamlets), David still pops in for tea and patiently listens to my odd complaint.

In the time I have spent with David, I have come to understand what I believe makes David's work so compelling and, in a sense, inextricable from the architect himself. They are the eclectic sensibilities he brings to his work. Son of a diplomat from Ghana, David's youth was spent in East Africa and in the Middle East, with a considerable amount of time spent traveling in between. Much of his inspiration to become an architect comes from this early exposure and influence. These days, he continues to feed his sense of aesthetic through travel—the spiritual resonance from a retreat in Japan to the natural beauty of the Sri Lankan landscape and the mud buildings in Yemen.

Then there is the international art scene that David has become known to inhabit. Though it is true he has designed houses for

some British artists including Chris Offili, David is an artist in his own right and, continuing on from his early days at art school, he still garners inspiration from this world. For his master's degree, he chose the Royal College, not only to study architecture but also to be surrounded by artists. There, in this socially diverse world, David remains rooted and, through his close connection with this world of "pure art," he clearly takes the creation of space from an artist's perspective, with the backing ideology that the two "arts" often run parallel, for example, in the sculptural aspects.

But then, for David, architecture is clearly not only about beauty, glamour and pop culture. Indeed, he views his work through the eyes of a multicultural artist. But perhaps most admirably, he is an architect with a social conscience, who today finds that he is most deeply motivated by wider social projects. The idea of communicating to many different levels of society within the framework of one structure, for him, has become a great challenge. Not only is there a task of imbuing his own sense of aesthetic on a large scale, but also fulfilling his growing sense of duty to the wider public, with the ultimate desire to serve a cross-cultural, multigenerational and diverse socioeconomic population.

These days, it seems like David is a man on a mission. Though working within his unique principles of design with an attitude of consummate professionalism, he still remains flexible within the awareness that he will never be able to please everyone. But when I ask David what his next step is in his career as an architect, he responds—once again with an eye on social concerns—that he would love to become a role model for black youth. And although he does not want to be labeled as a "black architect," the message he would like to pass on is that one does not have to be born on the right side of the world to make a cultural mark on it.

Previous page: David Adjaye among architecture books at his kitchen table of his own design. A series of black-and-white abstract paintings on the back wall are by London artist Henna Nadeem.
Opposite: A reclining chair in the drawing room/study/bedroom by Le Corbusier is David's passion. Stacks of architecture books serve as a table between two box-like chairs, the lighter wood chair is David's design.
Next pages, left: Detail of a model for a commercial building David designed in Battersea.
Next pages, right: Model of David's summer house retreat in Accra, Ghana.

Who are your favorite heroes in real life?
All the good guys.

Who are your favorite characters in history?
People who have stood for their beliefs.

What to your mind would be the greatest of misfortunes?
Lack of honest friends.

Who is your favorite writer?
Different every month.

What do you most value in your friends?
Honesty.

What is the quality you most admire in a woman?
Women who are able to be proud.

What is the quality you most admire in a man?
Men who are able to be humble.

Who is your favorite musician?
Different every week.

What is your most marked characteristic?
Saying "yes" too much.

What is your favorite color?
It changes every season.

KIM HERSOV

BY MICHAEL KORS

Hitchcock and humor…what a combo. When I first met Kim Hersov in New York many years ago, I was immediately struck by her icy blonde good looks. She had this Hitchcock heroine thing about her. Then I got to know Kim and realized the cool, chic exterior hid a terrific sense of humor and warmth. Ultimately, it's the mix of things that always intrigues me, not all one or the other.

When I was starting my business in New York and needed help addressing a zillion invitations to my show one night, meticulousness was a given, but, let's be honest, if you need to stay up working all night you need to laugh at the insanity of it all. Kim not only pitched in to help, but did so with a ruler at hand (God forbid a name was crooked on the envelope) and a great sense of humor. She is always the perfect blend with the best style. Kim and her family live with this blend every day. It's the way she dresses too…elegant, simple, chic, easy and, most importantly, never forced. Half the battle is not letting anyone see the hard work; make them think it's all a breeze.

Other than addressing envelopes for me on the side, Kim started in fashion as assistant editor in New York at *Vogue*, and has continued her career in London at *Harper's & Queen*. There are two things that strike me about Kim's career in fashion: 1. "Editor" sums up Kim's attitude towards fashion as well as the way she lives. She's all about distilling the best and leaving the rest. 2. She's seen it all: from packing slews of garment bags to traveling the globe—hardworking, yet always at ease is how I think of Kim. Sporty, California girl marries dashing, South African guy and sets up house in London. Allegra Hicks, a great friend of Kim's, walked into the house and immediately said how much it reminded her of San Francisco. San Francisco is a great analogy for Kim's home; it feels sporty and uncluttered, traditional yet light, calm yet there is always something going on.

Kim has a terrific-looking screen in her drawing room that came

Previous page: *Harper's & Queen* Editor at Large Kim Hersov in her dining room, wearing an evening gown by Velasco Andersson. On the mantle sit two terra-cotta Han tomb figures, above which hangs a 19th-century Regency gilt mirror. The table is set to entertain with tortoise shell chargers and cut crystal.
Above, left: Kim and youngest son, Luke Hersov, in the drawing room in front of an 18th-century Japanese painted paper screen given to Kim by her grandmother. The mirror above the fireplace is one of a pair of Italian paneled mirrors, 18th century.
Above, right: Kim seated in the outside terrace garden designed by Martin Summers. Indian mirrored arches hang with large terra-cotta pots on the wooden trellis.
Opposite: Alexander Hersov in the playroom with a painted wall mural from *The Jungle Book*, by Rudyard Kipling.
Next pages: Rob Hersov with Luke in the garden square in front of their house.

from her grandmother's house. She used the screen as a focal point in the room the same way she would wear a great looking Marni coat, blending it with low-key pieces so you get a totally unaffected look.

Another favorite place is where Kim's two boys have their own piece of Rob's South Africa and Kim's Trader Vic's tropicalia perfectly mixed in their little thatched cottage playroom. Her love of the mix comes from her grandmother, the gumption and spirit of Auntie Mame crossed with the chic of Babe Paley.

Nan Kempner, New York hostess, fundraiser extraordinaire, and an old friend of Kim's family from San Francisco, entertains with two round tables in her dining room rather than one grand table. Kim instinctively saw that even the most formal dining room could feel more relaxed this way. "I like to think of modern iconic things like Billy Baldwin, furniture, corduroy, camel hair and straw used in unexpected ways." Elegance without ease can be so old-fashioned.

I had lunch with Kim in London on one of those rare blazing hot days, when all of London is suddenly crimson red from a quick fry in the sun. In the blaze of the heat, in strides Kim—eight and a half months pregnant, looking cool as a cuke in a little short navy pique shift (Michael Kors, of course), giving the room a real burst of cool air. Once again, she reminded me that easy does win every time out.

Where would you like to live?
Wherever my family is (preferably where the sun shines).

To what faults do you feel most indulgent?
Always needing to be in control.

Who are your favorite heroes of fiction?
The Hobbit, Bilbo Baggins, and Frodo from
The Lord of the Rings.

Who is your favorite hero in real life?
Colin Powell is my man of the moment.

Who are your favorite characters in history?
Napoléon and Joséphine.

Who is your favorite painter?
Balthus.

Who is your favorite writer?
William Faulkner.

What is the quality you most admire in a man?
Integrity.

What is the quality you most admire in a woman?
Integrity.

What is your favorite virtue?
Generosity of spirit.

What is your favorite occupation?
The one I have—Editor at Large of *Harper's & Queen.*

What is your most marked characteristic?
Diplomacy.

What do you most value in your friends?
Loyalty.

What to your mind would be the greatest of misfortunes?
Loss of family.

What is your favorite color?
It depends on my mood: camel, cream, olive,
chocolate brown, red and robin's egg blue.

What is your favorite bird?
Swan.

ASHLEY
AND ALLEGRA HICKS

BY HAMISH BOWLES

It is a classic Chelsea street where pristine mid-nineteenth-century houses of gray brick smartly picked out in white are lined up in martial order in defiance of the messy confusion and retail chaos of nearby King's Road. Traditional flowering chintz cottons bloom at practically every window but one. In this renegade establishment, the tall sash windows are hung with thickly woven stuff the color of dead shrimp. The fabric's crescents of dull silver represent bulls' horns, the crest of Lord Mountbatten, a clue to the owners' identity.

These curtains were designed in 1935 by the chic modernist Marion Dorn and hung in the entrance gallery of the glamorous Park Lane penthouse (one of the first of its kind in the city) of Mountbatten and his chic wife Lady Edwina. That couple's flair for visual fireworks (*Vogue* noted that Lady Edwina's bedroom featured "snapdragon yellow walls" and a sofa upholstered in pale blue lambskin), married to that of their son-in-law, the legendary decorator David Hicks, has been inherited by their grandson Ashley Hicks. Ashley and his dynamically stylish wife, Allegra, have transformed their classic London manse into a temple to their idiosyncratic tastes and a crowded showplace for the results of their tireless design energies. The tone is set in the entrance hall.

Here, a fifties Italian glass mirror suggests Allegra's roots (she was raised in Turin, that conservative northern Italian bastion where great store has traditionally been set on quality and craftsmanship in the decorative arts). The mirror has been set against wallpaper that Ashley designed with cunningly intertwining twin As. The conventional banister was torn out and replaced by Tom Dixon with his brutalist galvanized steel example. The work of other whimsically

Ashley and Allegra Hicks, in their drawing room, sit on opposite ends of a small French settee, early 19th century, which belonged to Ashley's grandmother, Lady Edwina Mountbatten. A large red ceremonial feather hat from Cameroon hangs underneath a watercolor by Anish Kapoor, given by the artist to the Hickses as a wedding present. Both the carpet, "Spheres" dhurrie, and the "Flame Table," of parchment with burnished copper legs, were designed by Allegra.

What do you regard as the lowest depth of misery?
Rugger in the mud at public school.

Where would you like to live?
Villa Lante, Bagnaia.

What is your idea of earthly happiness?
Feeling the warm breeze through the marble screens of Shah Jahan's apartments in the Red Fort, Delhi.

To what faults do you feel most indulgent?
Nostalgia.

Who are your favorite heroes of fiction?
P.G. Wodehouse's Psmith and the man with the banana breakfast in Pynchon's *Gravity's Rainbow*.

Who are your favorite heroes in real life?
My wife and my children.

Who are your favorite characters in history?
Emperor Rudolf II, a dreamer; Doge Enrico Dandolo, a shit.

Who is your favorite painter?
Andrea Mantegna.

Who is your favorite writer?
Angelica Hicks, age 9.

What is the quality you most admire in a man?
Restraint.

What is the quality you most admire in a woman?
Elegance.

What is your most marked characteristic?
Incapacitating shyness.

What is your principal defect?
Rudeness.

What to your mind would be the greatest of misfortunes?
Blindness.

What is your favorite color?
Dirty pink.

What is your favorite bird?
Golden pheasant.

Pages 34-35: On top of a side table is a jet interior proposal by interior designer David Hicks, Ashley's father, done for a private client, 1968, with orange, yellow and pink tweed seats. The faux granite painted table top by Allegra houses a collection of small opium boxes from Jaisalmer. The little black box is Burmese, a present to Ashley from his father.

minded contemporary designers—among them Andre Dubreuil, Garouste and Bonetti, Borek Sipek and Danny Lane—recurs through the house. The Hickses would like more of their contemporaries' work, but as Ashley playfully admits "love to, but no room!" Small wonder: the indefatigable Hickses' design empire now extends to furniture, carpets, textiles, interiors and fashion. This giddily inventive and industrious world is showcased not only throughout their house, but also in their appropriately named book *Design Alchemy* and in Allegra's first shop, set in pretty Chelsea Green where, coincidentally, her father-in-law once established himself in trade.

The downstairs dining room is a testament to Allegra's skills as a trompe-l'œil artist. Here, she worked with her friend Mario Penati, with whom she studied this craft, to create an effective illusion of translucent curtains of Turkoman design drifting in an imagined breeze, revealing aerial views of castles in Ireland (a country that Ashley loves) surreally trapped within glass vitrines.

In the drawing room above, unexpected juxtapositions set the scene. Sir Arthur Cope's swaggering portrait of Edward VII in his Garter robes dominates the room, but somehow the flash of dark crimson in the monarch's sash manages to harmonize with the painting's unconventional neighbors, Coptic fragments and fragile Anish Kapoor works on paper among them. A polite giltwood eighteenth-century sofa is given new life via some gutsy Indian fabric upholstery. Above it, a characteristically Hicksian composition comprises an elegantly reductive work by Kapoor (the artist's wedding present to the couple) hanging over an extraordinary feathered headdress from Cameroon that seems like a fiery sunset of blazing scarlet feathers. Potent Basquiat crayon portraits flank the arrangement. Other artist friends represented here include Langlands & Bell (with whom Ashley once shared a studio), Donald Baechler (with whom Allegra once worked, and whose portrait of her captures and exaggerates her already dramatic Dietrich features), Francesco Clemente, Adam Fuss, James Brown, Julia Condon and Chris Offili. Ashley designed the room's Klismos chair and the iron drum table, as well as a cabinet to display a prized set of miniature Regency plaster casts of the Parthenon friezes, whilst Allegra designed the coffee table and consoles, their vellum shelves supported on scorched bronze branches like the leaves of the agave. Allegra's too is the porridge-colored Indian kilim. "Spheres" she calls it, with its interlocking bubbles traced in deep red, ivory and black. In the adjoining library, aesthetic rather than literary skills are demanded of the prospective reader as most of the books have been denuded of their dust jackets and are ranged, not alphabetically, but instead in dramatic color gradations according to their bindings. The effect, if bewildering to the novitiate, is nevertheless ravishing to the eye. The Hickses' eldest daughter, Angelica, has inherited these bookish instincts, her own tomes forming pyramidal still lifes around her room. Her equally enchanting sister Ambrosia (and as her godfather, I here declare an interest) favors aesthetic effects.

The library table has been trompe'd by Allegra with a map of the world that appears to be a tour de force of marquetry work; it also indicates the route of her honeymoon journey through India and Bali. This voyage of discovery sealed the couple's inherited passion for India (Mountbatten, of course, was the country's last Viceroy), and many of their design projects ensure that they continue to spend time there. Ashley has designed and produced jewelry there; Allegra, rugs, embroideries and textiles.

Ashley was brought up in a house around the corner, where his father's decorating conceits ran to lugubrious tinted glass windows and drawing room walls lacquered the color of Coca-Cola. Trained as an architect, he has inherited his father's instincts for elegant and dramatically symmetrical compositions, and for artful "tablescapes," a convention that Hicks père, no slouch in the self-promotion department, claimed, with some authority, to have conceived and refined. Ashley and Allegra's color sense, however, is noticeably more subtly nuanced. The brilliant pungency that characterized David Hicks's signature schemes is suggested in a presentation design for the interior of a private plane (sunflower, marigold, jade) that his son has placed in a

This page, top left: Allegra Hicks's sketch of a dress, "Sonia with Obi belt," from her summer collection, 2002. Top right: On a drawing room side table, covered with a Northern Indian embroidered cloth, a painting of daughter Angelica Hicks's feet by Samantha McEwen. The painted wood final prototype was designed by Ashley. Center right: The dining room walls, designed by Ashley, painted by Allegra, depict Turkish velvet curtains revealing cityscapes and vitrines with country house models. The étagère was designed by Ashley for his Jantar Mantar furniture collection. The chairs are from a set of Regency chairs belonging to Ashley's grandmother.

Bottom left: A 1920s German walnut dining table sits in front of the fireplace hearth designed by André Dubreuil of copper and metal, the mantle painted faux marble by Allegra. Julia Condon portraits of Allegra and Angelica rest on the mantle next to a Japanese Noh theater mask.

Next pages, left: Ashley rests his hand on the back of the "Klysmos" chair. Both the chair and small drum table in foreground are of his design. A portrait of Edward VII by Arthur Cope hangs on the wall above the sofa; to the left is a watercolor by Anish Kapoor.

Next pages, right: In the drawing room, fresh-cut flowers adorn a Milanese marquetry side table, 1790s. A copy of the nose from Michelangelo's *David* lies alongside a bowl made of pressed zucchini slices. Roman oil and scent bottles underneath a plexiglass case were a gift from Ashley to Allegra.

tablescape of his own invention. Ashley and Allegra's favorite color schemes suggest instead the spoils of their beloved Jaipur spice and jewel markets: the deep pinks of Burmese rubies, poisonous peridot greens, urinous topaz yellows and resonant amethyst mauves, together with cinnamon, saffron, paprika and sage. If there is a certain tonal restraint to Ashley and Allegra's artful scheming, their bedroom breaks the rule, erupting with sudden sixties exuberance in homage to David Hicks. Here, the bed is tented *à la polonaise* with a sprigged coral pink Fortuny print, its canopy swagged and crowned (in cocoa and *café au lait* cottons) like a mediaeval tent on the Field of the Cloth of Gold. The windows, once hung with saris from the Punjab (long since shattered in the unexpected London sun), are now curtained in one of Allegra's Tree of Life prints, and the dhurrie underfoot is woven with vivid ziggurats of pink and plum.

Ashley, who completed his father's posthumously published final book, *My Kind of Garden*, has recently written *David Hicks, Designer*, an overview of his father's work in the sixties and seventies, the period when it reached its flamboyant apogee. He has also reedited a range of the distinctively Op Art carpets with which his father embellished his bravura decorating projects. Despite these overt homages, however, Ashley Hicks's own emphatic tastes, married to those of Allegra, have forged to create a universe of style that is uniquely their own.

SOPHIE HAMILTON

BY ALANNAH WESTON

Once upon a time, long long ago (well, it was the seventies), in a far-off land, there lived a little girl called Sophie. She lived in a very big house overlooking a lake in a magical valley (actually it was a rather damp valley, but very green) with her mother and father and two brothers. And every day she would go down to the woods to look for fairies. She would crouch down very small (which wasn't easy, because she was tall for her age) and wait and wish and hope that they would appear. They never did, but the dream of them stayed with her till she grew up and became an emerald-eyed, raven-haired willow tree of a girl with legs and eyelashes that went on and on forever.

The grown-up Sophie lived at the top of a very tall house in a very trendy part of London. She wore corduroy blouson jackets with patches on the elbows and ivory cobweb dresses from the market. And on her long and slender feet (which she inherited from her long and slender father), she wore stripy trainers or silver slippers with the tiniest heels. The place where she lived was like incense (though it didn't smell that way). It was tawny and rich with soft matted carpets and ochre sinking sofas. Her boudoir was a real boudoir perched high above the room and wrapped in floating bits of crimson voile. Sophie's kitchen was lavender and immaculate. From her mother, who was very exotic, Sophie got her love of gypsy music and Ballets Russes, and an enigmatic smile. From her father, Sophie got a very naughty glint in her eyes and a love of skipping.

Now one of the things that Sophie had always wanted to do was to work with children. She studied psychology and learned how to reach them by releasing their imaginations. Then she went to Beirut, where she worked in a home for children with special needs. She told them stories and made up games for them. When she returned to London, she used art and drama to tune in to the imaginary worlds of children who needed badly to be understood.

One day, when she came home from work, she looked out of the window of her very tall house and sighed a very beautiful sigh (for Sophie is the best at sighing). Then she picked up her little red slip of a phone and called a friend she'd known since childhood. "Alannah-lu," she said (her diminutives are always sweetly phonetic). "I just don't think there's enough magic in the world." This was certainly true and I said so. Then Sophie told me her dream of a magic world for children. There, they flew on gossamer wings instead of silver scooters. Their playmates were fairies and goblins instead of Malibu Barbie. They wore pique cotton dresses trimmed with marabou instead of Gap Kids dungarees. They had silver wands instead of Sega joysticks.

For the other thing that had always captivated Sophie was the magic of beautiful things. When she was seventeen, she worked for a couturier in Paris, and she remembered the atelier as a trove of glittering beads, gold thread and swatches of intense color. She had been amazed by the miraculously fine handwork—pieces of crystal embroidered on wisps of tulle, perfectly real flowers sculpted from silk, onyx beads sewn onto heavy velvet. That Christmas, she made a fairy dress for her goddaughter, who was five. It was hand sewn from

Previous page: Lady Sophie Hamilton leans on the wrought iron balcony of her bedroom landing wearing a pair of fairy wings of her design and a dress she found in the flea market. The pattern on the curtain was designed by Ashley Hicks.

Opposite: An oil painting of a ballerina's corset by artist Thomas Fougeirol rests against the wall of Sophie's bedroom. In the foreground, a box of fairy wings Sophie designed for her company, Little Wings.

This page, top: Detail of bookcase lined with invitations and filled with books on fairies. The photograph is of Sophie and her brother as children in their grandmother's garden in Henley.

Middle: A fairy of Lady Cottington's Pressed Fairy Book by Angelica Cottington, Sophie's inspiration.

Below: Stenciled avocado green walls with tulip motif designed by Allegra Hicks and artist Mario Penati surround Sophie in her guest room. Sophie wears a silk dress of her own design.

Next page: On Sophie's dressing table, a silver mirror belonging to her Russian great-grandmother, next to a photo of her mother and grandmother. Various brooches lie next to a diamanté necklace.

crushed metallic silk the color of antique silver under a film of finest tulle. A cluster of crystal teardrops were sewn by hand onto each shoulder. Underneath was a satin petticoat with matching silver slippers. When she put it on with the organza wings, she told her mother she was sure she could fly.

It wasn't long before Sophie's boudoir was adrift in marabou feathers and tinsel strands, her car piled high with tiny catalogues, and her long white fingers raw from shaping wings out of silver wire. For Sophie's romantic nature was underpinned by passion. And her passion was grounded by a hidden toughness—the kind that doesn't suffer fools (or late suppliers). I watched, amazed, as if by magic "Little Wings" took flight.

Sophie still runs her fairy empire from her flat in Notting Hill. She floats through London like an enigmatic swan (or skips absurdly down Oxford Street at two in the morning). But she is happiest in the green valley in Ireland where she grew up with her father and mother and two brothers. And it is there, I'm sure, that she will live happily ever after.

Next page, left: View of London's Notting Hill from Sophie's drawing room window.
Next page, right: A portrait of Sophie in a dress of her own design. The yellow fabric on the walls was designed by Allegra Hicks.

What do you regard as the lowest depth of misery?
To lose or be separated from the people closest to me.

Where would you like to live?
Nirvana.

What is your idea of earthly happiness?
Feeling at home in my own skin.

To what faults do you feel most indulgent?
Tears of joy and sadness.

Who are your favorite heroes of fiction?
Ursula Brangwen, Lara (Dr. Zhivago).

Who are your favorite heroes in real life?
Nelson Mandela, Uliana Lopatkina (prima ballerina in the Kirov).

Who are your favorite characters in history?
Jesus, Nelson and Emma, Carl Jung.

Who is your favorite painter?
Eugène Delacroix, Auguste Rodin, Amedeo Modigliani, Henri Cartier-Bresson!

Who is your favorite musician?
Tony Maroni.

Who are your favorite writers?
Ivan Turgenev, William Butler Yeats, D.H. Lawrence.

What is the quality you most admire in a man?
Compassion.

What is the quality you most admire in a woman?
Grace.

What is your favorite virtue?
Honesty.

What is your favorite occupation?
Riding, dancing, ten-pin bowling.

Who would you have liked to be?
One of the great ballerinas.

What is your most marked characteristic?
Openness.

What do you most value in your friends?
Loyalty.

What is your principal defect?
Over-analytical of other people.

What to your mind would be the greatest of misfortunes?
To be unaware.

What is your favorite color?
Red.

What is your favorite bird?
The ugly duckling.

WILL STANHOPE AND
CANDIDA BOND

BY NICKY HASLAM

Picture this: a column-fronted, pale gray granite house, the lochs and woods of its park rolling away to a wild seashore, in that surprisingly douce and oddly level part of the Highlands above Aberdeen. Inside, behind windows and doorcases of monumental scale, what first takes the breath away is an immense atrium, full story height, topped by a shimmering glass dome. Daylight floods down into this neo-classical hall, presently empty, but easy to imagine as a sculpture gallery. Beyond, to left and right, the currently bare walls of the enfilade of rooms— there are sixty-seven at last count—one can envisage as the perfect setting for huge pictures or sets of important tapestries. But for the moment there is just space, and silence. Outside, white doves noiselessly circle a stone dovecote.

Suddenly, a mahogany door swings open, and, with the unmistakable sound of a jigsaw whirring through MDF, a slight figure in paint-spattered, faded blue jeans, her blonde hair gleaming in the shafts of sunlight, runs into the hall. The door clunks shut. Silence again. Then the girl, by now quite close, speaks. "Isn't this wonderful? Can you believe it's my home?" Candida says.

Well, you can't and you can. I mean, this vast house in this idyllic setting, miles from anywhere, lost between the woods and the water, beginning to be brought to life by this beautiful waif, is the stuff of fairy tales. And yet it's real; the jigsaw's whine is Will Stanhope making bookshelves, Candida's jeans are not paint, but clay spattered. For besides being the lovely "face" of the Chanel Allure perfume, frequently whizzing to Paris to be with Karl Lagerfeld for the opening, say, of his jewelry boutique in Place Vendôme, and with fellow model Saffron Aldridge and

The Honorable Mr. and Mrs. Stanhope stand in the dining room of the small London flat, once Will's bachelor pad, in front of a drawing of Elvaston Castle, the Stanhope family castle in Derbyshire.

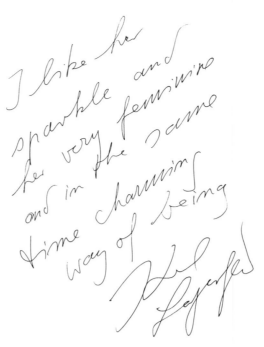

I like her sparkle and her very feminine and in the same time charming way of being

Karl Lagerfeld

fashion editor Kim Hersov, "ambassadors" for Chanel's new Brompton Cross store, Candida is a accomplished sculptor ("I keep my clay in the old ice-house in the park; it's the perfect temperature") with a upcoming exhibition at the Sladmore Gallery in London. "But this house is my main job right now."

"It was amazing how the Chanel thing happened. Right out of the blue. I was at my parents' house in Gloucestershire, on my sculpting machine thing, and my mobile rang. I had to run to the top of the nearest hill to get a clear line. It was a French girl's voice saying Chanel had seen a tiny ad in *Vogue* for one of my exhibitions, and that I was being considered for 'a campaign.' So I sent some happy snaps; they rang back saying 'you're no. 1 choice.' Then they rang and said I wasn't, and I sort of forgot about it. Then finally the call saying I was IT, come to Paris now."

Luckily, when that call came, Will and Candida were not up a mountain in Ethiopia, or trekking the Mexican jungle. "He likes to be doing something adventurous, or making things. He's a dab hand with a Stanley knife. Maybe they should be renamed Stanhope knives…" On cue, the door swings open again, and Will appears, covered from head to toe in sawdust. "Cand, I've made that plinth for your big piece, it'll look great in the middle of the atrium, don't you think? Can't we all have a cup of tea?"

"Oh, Will, you know how much I hate cooking; let's have a drink instead." So wine glasses in hand, we walk through the darkening rooms, both explaining how here there's going to be this picture, there the requisite tapestries. Will and Candida are fortunate to have inherited from his father's former house furniture of the scale needed. But that's yet to come. At the moment, there's just a huge shabby sofa, and until Will installs the electrics, no lights or sound system. This matters not a jot to this radiantly happy pair, so obviously content in this faraway place with each other's company. Will pulls his guitar from under the sofa, Candida rummages for her flute. And by the firelight, they curl up together and start playing a gentle riff…

Candida asked me to write this piece "because you've known me all my life." It's true, I have, though to me it seems mere moments since she was a tennis-mad teen, or a twenty-something hopelessly trying to make roast lamb for Van Morrison in a cottage near my house in Hampshire, let alone seconds since her gloriously romantic summer wedding…but I only hope I will know Candida and Will for the rest of mine.

TAMARA AND
MATTHEW MELLON II

BY WILLIAM CASH

"I don't like men who look too fashionable," says the designer-shoe tycoon Tamara Mellon of her debonair husband, Matthew T. Mellon II, scion of the influential East Coast banking and oil family, whose surname is synonymous on both sides of the Atlantic with philanthropy and four generations of social style. "I'm not sure I'll ever get the WASP look completely out of his system," she adds, casting a quick glance across the San Lorenzo lunch table at her husband's pale blue button-down poplin shirt. "He looks best just the way he is, except that I'm now taking him to get his suits made by Doug Hayward in Mayfair. But Matthew still loves his Brooks Brothers boxer shorts. That I will never be able to change."

Matthew, a venture capitalist who was brought up in Manhattan, Palm Beach and Maine, and graduated from the Wharton business school in 1989, can be forgiven for finding it occasionally hard, now that he has made his home in London, to discard aspects of his blue-blood American background. After all, his uncle did coin the term WASP. His family founded the Mellon Bank, Gulf Oil and Carnegie Mellon University, the investment bank Drexel Burnham, America's National Gallery—and that's just the men. His grandmother was a trustee of the Museum of Modern Art in New York and, to trump it all, his great-aunt Katherine Drexel was canonized as a saint by Pope John Paul II in 2000.

Yet, in this very modern style of Mellon marriage, which took place in May 2000 at a society-wedding-of-the-year extravaganza at Blenheim Palace, it is his beautiful and dynamic wife, Tamara, née Yeardye, the Lady Diana Cooper of London's new

Opposite: Tamara and Matthew Mellon II, and their dog Biscuit, a Brussels Griffin, in the drawing room of their Belgravia flat.
Next page, left: A detail of a shoe design for Jimmy Choo. Right: Tamara, with Biscuit, seated in her dressing room closet among rows of Jimmy Choo shoes.

Bright Young Things, who has been grabbing the headlines as a twenty-first-century empire builder. Their white-tie wedding for 300 guests left even the combined ranks of *Tatler* and *Vogue*'s jejeune social writers—the paparazzi were left caged up outside—swooning as they felt the sheer wattage of A-list heat on display at the stately Oxfordshire home of the Duke of Marlborough. But not even the presence at the packed church of Elizabeth Hurley and Hugh Grant, a few days just after they had announced their split, could turn any attention away from the stunning bride, dressed in Valentino.

From its modest beginnings in 1996 with one small shop in Motcombe Street, off Bond Street, in which Tamara happily "served the customers, designed the collection, cleaned the shop and did the shipping," Jimmy Choo now has branches in London, Beverly Hills, Las Vegas, New York and 150 speciality stores around the world. In 2000, Jimmy Choo won British Accessory Designer of the Year.

Tamara got the idea for founding the bespoke designer shoe brand while Accessory Editor at *Vogue* in London. "I was taught how to predict trends and styles," she says. She saw an opening for chic and exclusive shoes and approached the Malaysian shoemaker Jimmy Choo, who operated from a modest workshop in London's East End, about placing him on the world fashion stage. Her creative director is Sandra Choi, Jimmy Choo's niece. "We took the name and turned it into a luxury brand," says Tamara. "By developing small boutiques in London and in the United States, we institutionalized the name. Our aim is to make shoes that look younger and sexy, and we try to be always on the right side of sexy. It's a very fine line."

Nowadays, the Oscar ceremony in Los Angeles has become a virtual advertorial catwalk for Jimmy Choo, with stars like Madonna among Tamara's best clients. But when she started out in 1996, it was Princess Diana who really helped launch the

"Ricky" AW2001 Sandra Choi for Jimmy Choo.

Jimmy Choo style. "Whenever Diana was upset, she'd order dozens of shoes," says Tamara. "And that happened quite a lot. She used to drive up to the shop herself, no bodyguards, and just walk in."

While Tamara may speak with a cut-glass Diana Cooper accent, and enjoys the legendary 1930s English society beauty's delicious looks to match, her own background is, if anything, more Mid-Atlantic than her American venture capitalist husband's. Her father, Tom Yeardye, was the brains (and C.E.O.) behind the hairdressing salon Vidal Sassoon, and moved her family to Beverly Hills, where she lived from 1976 until 1983, when he sold the company and they moved back to London. He helped with the financial backing of Jimmy Choo. Tamara's mother was the Chanel No. 5 model in the 1960s and early 1970s.

While Mellons have often wed European society girls—Matthew's grandmother is German—marrying into the Mellon family was previously usually a pretext for a woman giving up any notions of a career. Not so for Tamara. "Matthew's uncle said to me that I was more like the old timers in his family, who worked hard. That's not to say Matthew doesn't, because he is always very busy. He's constantly researching funds and taking meetings with people, but he doesn't have a conventional sort of job. I didn't marry Matthew as an opportunity to give up work," she says. If one is to summarize their contrasting work ethics, it might be fair to say that Tamara's is more self-made American, while her husband's is conversely more in tune with his aristocratic British friends.

This has its mutual benefits. The Matthew Mellons can travel together when Tamara is required to be abroad on Jimmy Choo business. But though Matthew cuts a dash accompanying Tamara to, say, dinner with her close friend Valentino in Paris, the no-nonsense WASP does admit to having a "love-hate" relationship with Italy, where Tamara often has to visit to supervise production. "Factory hopping is really not my thing," he says with characteristic Mellon candor.

Matthew and Tamara first met properly—after a false start at a gathering in London—at the wedding of Matthew's close friend Henry Dent-Brocklehurst, heir to Sudeley Castle in Gloucestershire. Henry and Matthew had previously lived together in Los Angeles during the 1990s in Henry's aesthetically challenged moated faux castle Hollywood Hills bungalow. After the Dent-Brocklehurst wedding, Matthew offered Tamara a lift back to London in the back of a friend's car, sharing the back seat with Elizabeth Hurley. "When I jumped in the back of the car with Tamara, I knew I had two and a half hours to close the deal," says Matthew. "And I knew those were going to be the most important two and a half hours of my life."

Never known to do anything in his life by halves, Matthew then took her out to dinner three nights in a row at the Mimo D'Ischia restaurant in Belgravia. "I always wanted to marry a European girl, because I find their taste and style more refined and laid-back," says Matthew. "If somebody asked me if I was ever going to marry a shoe designer, I would have said 'never in a thousand years.' When I met Tamara, I thought she was the most settled, most confident person in the world, and that's what I wanted as a wife. When all the world has gone to hell in a basket, my wife is a pillar of strength and calmness. She doesn't react to it with emotions, she reacts to it with solutions. That's what I like about her."

Partly as a result of living such a high-pressure life in the fast lane of international fashion, the Mellons have deliberately chosen, with their interior designer friend Camilla Buchanan-Michaelson, to decorate their gracious London house with an eye away from fussy fashion detail to a look of elegant simplicity and "spiritual" comfort. Although their two-story Belgravia house lies in the social heartland of the original Bright Young Things of Evelyn Waugh and Diana Cooper's 1930s London, the location today is now Embassy-CCTV central, making them self-confessed social "lone rangers." This suits them

Clockwise, from top left: A mother-of-pearl inlaid mirror from Morocco hangs over the mantle in the front entry. Behind Tamara are two Rodin bronze figures on the side table. A framed memoriam of 3-cent United States stamp, together with a picture of Matthew's great-great-uncle, financier Andrew W. Mellon, Secretary of State, founder of the National Gallery in Washington. An 18th-century cabinet houses Tamara's collection of new and vintage handbags. Tamara sits in her kitchen in front of a photograph by Peter Beard, as Matthew stands before a carved pine bookcase designed by architect Detmar Blow, from the turn of the 19th century, and copied for the Duke of Westminster's estate from a bookcase on his yacht.

both—now that they are starting a family and their party days are over—just fine. "Nobody lives here," says Matthew. "Anybody who does soon moves to Notting Hill."

"I'm really quite a private person," adds Tamara. "I have the same close friends that I have always had, such as Emily Oppenheimer and Tamara Beckwith. I don't like going out. When I do, it is mostly for work."

The centerpiece of their imposing Belgravia drawing room reflects this spiritual inner order: a carved and gilted wooden Buddha head, which Tamara found in an antique shop on Walton Street. After the Buddha entered the room, her original idea of a simple cream and white color plan was emboldened by a shopping trip to Morocco, which made the house more colorful and exotic, reflecting Tamara and Matthew's own ever-expanding global signatures. The walls of the dining room are covered in waxed plaster.

Matthew was involved, for a while, in helping to design the Jimmy Choo men's show range, but has bowed out of his wife's global business to pursue his own business career as a venture capitalist. However, whether he is playing golf with Hugh Grant or having a new suit altered in the Mayfair tailor's fitting room of Doug Hayward, Matthew always has his mobile phone at hand, ready to provide "emotional support" to his wife, or just a useful phone number from his database of thousands. "I'm now an AOL Buddy List junkie," says Matthew, "which, these days, is just about my only vice."

Matthew Mellon II at his kitchen table in Belgravia.

What do you regard as the lowest depth of misery?
A drug addict living on the streets.

Where would you like to live?
London with Los Angeles weather.

To what fault do you feel most indulgent?
Shopping.

Who is your favorite hero of fiction?
Catwoman.

Who is your favorite character in history?
Elizabeth I.

Who is your favorite painter?
Van Gogh.

Who is your favorite musician?
Philip Glass.

Who is your favorite writer?
Antonia Fraser.

What is the quality you most admire in a man?
Good manners.

What is the quality you most admire in a woman?
Honesty.

What is your idea of earthly happiness?
A night in with my husband.

What is your favorite virtue?
Loyalty.

What is your favorite occupation?
My job.

Who would you have liked to be?
Cleopatra.

What is your most marked characteristic?
Patience.

What do you most value in your friends?
Loyalty.

What is your principal defect?
Procrastination.

What to your mind would be the greatest of misfortunes?
A young death.

What is your favorite color?
Turquoise.

What is your favorite bird?
A dove.

Tamara in a red Valentino dress, seated in the bedroom on a pink Dali-esque bench, 1950s Italian, looks adoringly at Biscuit. Behind her, an Andy Warhol lithograph of Princess Grace.

SELINA BLOW

BY AMICIA DE MOUBRAY

It has been a long time since a creature as exotic as Selina Blow inhabited the international fashion scene. Her sharply tailored coats in rich hues are beloved by a devoted clientele on both sides of the Atlantic. No one else could say, as she does, "I'm not crazy about pastels; it's slightly evident," and make it sound like an understatement while sitting in her midnight blue Notting Hill home: "It's like the witch's house."

A tall striking figure with a crop of jet-black hair severely cut in a dramatic fringe, she makes heads turn wherever she goes. Her strong sense of personal style permeates every facet of her life, from her trademark vivid red lipstick and the pointed leather boots she always wears, to her two dogs, a pair of black Scottish terriers endearingly called Maud and Myrtle–"I love their rather odd-looking angular features." In spite of the definitive visual statements she makes, she is almost cavalier about fashion. "I am not remotely interested in dictating fashion. I like timeless pieces, clean shapes you can wear with anything."

Selina is an excellent advertisement for her own clothes. Never to be seen without a signature coat, she elegantly demonstrates how infinitely flexible they are as garments. By day, she wears a coat combined with Jermyn Street men's shirts and whatever is not "in the wash" in the evening. "You can wear my clothes for gardening or for an evening at the opera." The look is at once effortless but clearly grandiose in both its conception and the wearing. Selina admits that there is a slightly tongue-in-cheek element to her philosophy.

Her love of color and fabrics can be ascribed to her mixed heritage of a Sri Lankan mother and an English father—

Designer Philip Treacy's straw hat "Madonna Rides Again" from his Couture collection tops his friend Selina Blow's head. She is wearing a blue quilted biker jacket of her own design.

combining the opulence of the East with finely tuned English tailoring. Her mother, a former catwalk model, met her father, Jonathan Blow, an English historian, at a charity show at Berkeley Castle.

"My mother was a great influence. Seeing her wearing Thea Porter and Bill Gibb in a remote part of Gloucestershire was very stimulating to a child's imagination." Her mother, Helga, now lives in her childhood home in Kandy, Sri Lanka, which she runs as a hotel, Helga's Folly. It is a heady blend of Sri Lankan exoticism, Buddhas, murals, furniture mixed with gold-embroidered cushions, black mosquito nets and four-poster beds. The hotel has a spectacular view overlooking Kandy.

"Although I work with a very diverse range of fabrics, including corduroy, Harris tweeds, velvets and brocades, my pieces are very recognizable—clean, lean tailoring with strong unusual fabrics. I don't like having things too categorized."

The interior of the commodious house she shares with her husband, Charles Levinson, a private doctor, and their three-year-old son, Augustus, and her two stepchildren, Bessy and Johnny, is imbued throughout with the strong Blow style. It is at once grand but irreverent. Selina and Charles have masterfully combined a richly eclectic mix of inherited pieces, such as an unusual black chinoiserie desk that belonged to her father, with Buddhas and incense burners from her maternal Sri Lanka, opulent English country house style sofas, and the odd item garnered from junk shops. "It's fun; it all works well together. Charles is very keen on shopping. I have to fill my car with cardboard boxes to prevent him buying more things for the house."

Joe Strummer, the lead singer in The Clash, previously owned the house. The dramatic midnight blue theme is continued inside, in a strong cocktail of theatrically rich deep blues and burgundy reds. "I have a passion for very strong pure colors and love the different tricks that light can play with color. It is so much easier to opt for dark strong color; it gives one greater freedom to have a more eclectic mix." There is not a whiff of the cool, pared-down interiors that are so popular with so many thirty-something fashion aficionados.

Perhaps surprisingly, Selina likens her job to Charles's in that they both deal with people intimately. "In fashion, you often see

Two Scottish terriers, Maud and Myrtle, share a seat next to the fire in the drawing rooms painted burgundy and electric blue.

a very private side to someone, how they perceive themselves. So our worlds may appear to be polar opposites, but we are able to share a great many experiences."

She had an extraordinary childhood at Hilles, a house designed by her grandfather, Detmar Blow, an Arts and Crafts architect. A handsome house, it stands perched high up on an escarpment overlooking the Vale of Gloucester to Wales in the far distance. It is not surprising that growing up in such dramatic surroundings, combined with her dual heritage, has spawned such a highly original individual. "As a child, I was rather isolated, which enabled me to create my own imaginary kingdom. I'm grateful for that. I was a shy child. My clothes were a form of armor."

Selina never rests on her laurels for a moment. "In my work, I feel like an Indian god with six hands." In addition to her womenswear and menswear, she has recently launched a childrenswear line. "I like the idea of miniatures. It is as if they are little tiny cakes."

Selina's imagination is endless.

This page: A black-and-white photograph from the sixties of Selina's grandfather, Sri Lankan ambassador to France, and Charles de Gaulle rests on the fireplace mantle next to old photograph postcards of Queen Elizabeth II. The large gilt frame holds a drawing of Selina's former storefront on Elizabeth Street; the smaller frames show Sri Lankan interiors. The standing Buddha is made of sandstone.
Below, left: Selina with her husband, Charles Levinson, and their son, Augustus, on the drawing room sofa. Behind them, a colorful wall hanging from Uzbekistan.
Below, right: Selina's grandfather's Chippendale writing desk. Next to the wooden seated Sri Lankan Buddha is a black-and-white photograph of Selina taken by Michael Roberts. Various coronation cups, a cross necklace of water sapphires and a twisted ginger root adorn the desk top.

CATHERINE PREVOST HEESCHEN

BY KATE REARDON

"Designing a home is not so different from designing a piece of jewelry," remarks American jewelry designer Catherine Prevost Heeschen. "You must consider the quality of materials, proportion and mood that you want to create." Luckily Catherine and her German entrepreneur husband, Andreas Heeschen, have similar taste. Both love Art Deco, Tamara de Lempicka paintings and Jean-Michel Frank furniture. Together with their collection of Buddha statues gathered on their numerous travels, these influences have resulted in a home combining sleek modern design with a more exotic sensuality.

After an epic renovation, the Heeschen's home has become a testament to their partnership. Although not quite the Taj Mahal, it's not far off. Andreas bought the house before they met and had originally planned it as a bachelor pad. But Cupid put an end to that. "He brought me here on our fifth date," says Catherine. "And in this room he said, 'I want you to spend the rest of your life with me and in this house.' So from that moment on, it's been ours."

Andreas then whisked Catherine off to Venice, flying her in his own twin engine plane. And the couple were married there one year later, on a romantic foggy winter night. The guests were decked in white tie and drank bellinis in a grand palazzo complete with Veronese painted ceilings.

The German-American partnership is a good one. Catherine, who went to school in New York and Boston, says, "I very much come from the East Coast ethic. But I think it's nice when you're married to someone from a different culture, because you're constantly coming from different angles." Her friends always knew that she would end up with a European man, and she admits, "I was always attracted to European men because they had a mysterious air about them."

A high-tech glass paneled entryway with frosted glass walkway and stainless steel balustrade were all crafted in Germany and brought to London by truck. Catherine Prevost Heeschen stands at the front door.

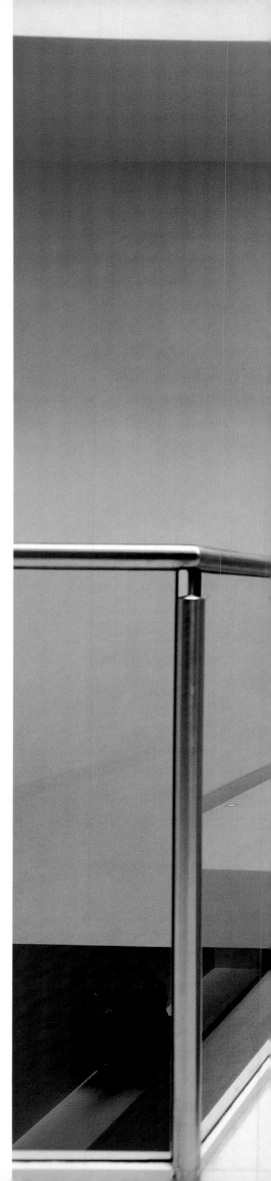

Catherine and Andreas's story has something of the thunderbolt about it. "When we met, I'd just arrived from New York. I was planning the opening of my shop, spent all my time with the builders and had no time to see him." Andreas's response has become the stuff of legend. She continues, "It was around Christmas, and the doorbell rang. I opened the door, and there was a very large man holding a huge Christmas tree with another man behind him holding all the ornaments. Andreas knew I was busy, so he sent over a full Christmas tree for me in my home. That's when my mother looked at me and said, 'You have to marry this man.'"

Since then, the couple has discovered a passion for hiking, and when not busy collecting Buddha heads in the Far East, they regularly slope off to various retreats and spas to indulge their rather vigorous hobby. It has taken them to Arizona, Colorado, Morocco and Switzerland, and their ambition is to hike in Tibet and Nepal. "There is nothing quite like climbing 12,000-foot mountains," says Andreas, "and finding hidden lakes and windswept valleys where there is not a soul in sight."

Built around 1910, the Heeschen's home retains the glamour of that era. "The only problem was that the rooms were too small, and there was no sense of space. So we knocked down walls and excavated to create a basement," says Catherine. The couple wanted to create a feeling of light and brought in Voit, a specialist team from Germany, to install glass panels throughout the house. Steel, glass and dark ebony wood were combined to create a modern, sleek atmosphere. Even the staircase, made from a single piece of steel, had to be brought in one piece from Germany.

Each piece of furniture has a story: the shagreen dining table, designed by the couple, was made in the Philippines, the Florentine onyx hall table was ordered on their honeymoon near the Pitti Palace in Florence, and even the garden's huge stone frieze was brought back from a trip to Bali.

As a contrast to the minimalism of the rest of the house, the drawing room is a cozier space. "We wanted one room that was very warm. That is why we covered the walls in mushroom Alcantara suede," says Catherine. Andreas also insisted on installing high-tech Lutron lighting in every room, a concept that initially underwhelmed Catherine, although she is now delighted. "It is such a thrill to walk in the door, push one button and watch the house come to life—it's very dramatic." Which prompted one guest to observe that were James Bond to grow up and get married, this is exactly the sort of house he'd live in. Fittingly, one of the Heeschen's favorite aspects is the video room, complete with Italian sofas and a vast flat-screen DVD unit that takes up most of the wall.

"Being from New York, my idea of a garden was Central Park," admits Catherine. "So I have loved learning about plants and choosing them for our first garden." The couple worked with a garden designer to achieve an exotic, jungle-like feel. "Even the willow tree had to go," she says, "as it made the garden very dark and sad. We wanted a light, modern garden." Now, paved with honey-colored French limestone and with a bamboo-edged wall, it feels considerably more Bali than Chelsea, with "not a traditional English trellis or rosebush in sight."

Catherine's success as a jewelry designer is due largely to the fact that she lives the life of her clients. She has become the poster girl for her own jewelry. "I don't design collections that aren't elegant, because I would never wear it, and I know my clients wouldn't either." Catherine's client list reads like a marketing man's dream and spans the best-dressed lists of New York, Hollywood and London. And she knows what they want. "I have noticed that they come to me for pieces that are whimsical yet opulent," she says, "like knuckle-duster cocktail rings or yards of tourmalines or rubies to wrap many times around their necks." Just as her jewelry is elegant and sophisticated, Catherine's taste in clothes is similarly chic. What most of us would save for best, she wears every day—scruffy is not a word in her style lexicon. Always groomed to perfection, her glossiness is typical Manhattan style, and tooth-grindingly envied by us natives.

Clockwise, from top left: Portrait of Catherine and Andreas Heeschen. Top, right: A detail of a shagreen jewelry box cabinet from the Philippines on top of a shagreen table top. Below, right: 1930s style low-back contemporary dining room chairs await the arrival of the dining table from the Philippines. A large frosted glass paned window with a black frame was made to match a similar sliding screen door. Below, left: An early 17th-century German depiction of St. Catherine of Alexandria hangs above the drawing room sofa. On either side are two brass lamps, 1970, from an estate sale in Las Vegas. The walls are upholstered in camel-colored Alcantara suede. Center, left: Catherine in her downstairs library at work with her jewelry, measuring a ring for size. A variety of semiprecious colored stones and beaded necklaces cover the table top.

COSIMA PAVONCELLI

BY CLAUS VON BÜLOW

The biographers of every Bright Young Thing in this book ought to declare their bias as a friend or as a professional judge of style, or in my case, as a parent. Is Cosima a "Bright Young Thing"? The first evidence that she was bright was at the Brick Church Nursery School in Manhattan. The 1971 Year Report described her as having star qualities, and was so nauseatingly laudatory that her mother and I immediately assumed that some benign Fairy (in the old-fashioned sense of the word) had switched her CV with that of the offspring of Albert Einstein and Greta Garbo. How reassuring for parents if all school reports could be edited by the School's fund-raiser rather than some martinet teacher. At the age of four, Cosima showed some signs of style. We asked her what color she would like in the nursery of our new summer home. "Purple," she answered without a moment's hesitation. I vaguely remembered that the Empresses of the late Roman empire were taken to a special porphyry-paneled room for the birth of their children. Imperial babes were consequently said to have been "born in the purple," a bit like our expression of being "born with a silver spoon in your mouth." Had Cosima, aged four, been surreptitiously reading my nine-volume edition of Gibbon's *Decline and Fall of the Roman Empire*, and had she therefore assumed that purple was just the right color for the nursery in a Newport cottage? "No," she answered, "purple is the color of my favorite lollipop, the cherry-flavored one."

The next step in our child's meteoric career was at the Bailey's Beach Sports Group, where she picked up every prize for basket-weaving, swimming, and a Sampras killer

Cosima Pavoncelli seated in the drawing room entrance. Above her is a small framed watercolor by Bonnard of an old man and an infant, given to her son, Nicolas, for his christening by his grandfather Claus von Bülow. Above the bureau is a life-size charcoal drawing of her husband, Riccardo, by artist Emma Sargent.

serve on the tennis court. When her mother declined to use the resultant loot of fake gold trophies as dinner-table decorations, Cosima learned that glory and fame have to be tempered with good taste and discretion.

In her grandmother's home, Cosima was, at an early age, exposed to the glittering ormolu on the many signed pieces of what we disrespectfully called FFF (Fine French Furniture). Here again, Cosima followed her mother in finding that the FFF "ébénistes" did not really make furniture suitable for "putting one's feet up," or as comfortable repositories for a quartet of Labrador puppies. During the ensuing decades, I have had occasion to admire Cosima's sense of style from her college rooms, "the empty-beer-can décor," to her present London home where her two small children make sure that every room looks thoroughly "lived in."

Cosima's mother was for several years on the official "Best Dressed List" and rightly so. When some glossy magazines in later years have included Cosima in their "Best Legs List" or "Best Dressed List," she has, I am sure, quietly thanked her mother for those very same legs and that sense of style. At a Parent's Day event at The Chapin School, I was once tackled by an irate and somewhat pretentious mother, "Why has Cosima got a French governess? She would find Spanish much more useful for speaking to her staff!" In my most obsequious voice, I replied that I was sure Cosima would be sweating in the kitchen over her own pots and pans, but would want to read L'Escoffier and Brillat-Savarin in the original. My interlocutor went off in a huff, mumbling that we were no doubt bringing Cosima up to be a Marxist. Cosima's mother and her half-sister, Ala, had both gone as boarders to St. Timothy's in Maryland. How to have a good seat on a horse was an important part of the curriculum for young ladies of quality. But Cosima, in her infinite wisdom on leaving Chapin, decided she wanted to see what boys were like. So she went off to Brook's, near North Andover, and a few years later took Route 95 down to Brown University. These were difficult years in the family, and because of her age, more so for Cosima. She learned that style is not a matter of how to compete with Mrs. Marcos's shoe closet, but of how to conduct yourself in adversity. Cosima showed great courage, and this was recognized by her

A large tropical palm and walls of ivy dominate the back garden terrace.
A blustery London day brings down the wet leaves.

friends and teachers in the love and support they gave her. After graduating from Brown, Cosima went on to get a master's in English Literature at London University, and also completed some courses at the Sorbonne and at the British Institute in Florence. When she first arrived in Tuscany, I took her to meet my old friend the historian Sir Harold Acton, whose villa La Pietra now belongs to the Institute of Fine Art of New York University. Harold expressed a little concern when he heard that Cosima was en route to visit Lord Lambton near Pisa, since this friend had single-handedly revived the reputation of Englishmen as great seducers. "He hasn't seen me since my christening," explained Cosima. Acton, whose appreciation of nubile young women was purely aesthetic, mumbled, "Well, he may just find you a little more interesting now."

Cosima became a talented freelance journalist in London, but she had fallen in love with Italy. The country not only teaches you style in the sense of how to wear a Verdura bracelet and how not to order a cappuccino after 11 A.M., it is the country where you learn to love everything that has made both Europe and America a treasure trove of culture and civilization. Every young girl should have a love affair with Aquinas, Dante, Giotto and St. Francis, then continue with Alberti, Botticelli, Leonardo and Michelangelo, Galileo and Columbus, down to Verdi, Garibaldi and Fermi. There is hardly anything of beauty and human thought in the last sixteen hundred years that was not born in Italy. No wonder that Cosima chose a dashing Italian, Riccardo Pavoncelli, a renowned condottiere-banker in London for her husband. Cosima's own genes are from an austere North–Scottish-American on her mother's side, Danish on mine. The infusion of the warm and civilizing South in the bloodline will be a blessing. To date, there are two puttis, Nicolas and Marina, worthy of inclusion on a Tiepolo canvas, and busy with their own crayons in improving their mother's décor.

What do you regard as the lowest depth of misery?
Sleep deprivation.

What is your idea of earthly happiness?
Sleeping late without guilt.

To what faults do you feel most indulgent?
Laziness.

Who is your favorite hero of fiction?
The Scarlet Pimpernel.

Who is your favorite hero in real life?
My father.

What is your principal defect?
Lack of confidence.

What is your favorite occupation?
Reading to my children before bed.

Who is your favorite painter?
John Singer Sargent.

Who is your favorite writer?
Henry James.

What is the quality you most admire in a man?
Courage.

What is the quality you most admire in a woman?
Courage.

What is your favorite virtue?
Kindness.

What do you most value in your friends?
Their support.

What is your favorite color?
Raspberry.

What is your favorite bird?
The seagull. It reminds me of
my childhood on the beach.

Above, left: An English needlepoint rug originally in Cosima's family home in New York graces the drawing room. An unusual warm London light glows through the two French doors.

Above, right: Iron balconies, wonderful glass bell jar lanterns and porticos make up the London street on which Cosima and her family live.

Below, left: A late-Victorian gilt convex mirror, a present from Cosima to Riccardo before they were married, hangs in the stairwell and reflects the glass conservatory Cosima uses as her office.

Below, right: Nicolas and Marina Pavoncelli in the drawing room. A painting of Nijinsky by Jean-Emile Blanche from his series *Les Orientales* hangs above the sofa. The steel bookcase with leather-bound books was originally in Claus von Bülow's New York study.

SAFFRON ALDRIDGE

BY ALAN ALDRIDGE

She got named Saffron. Other names were considered—Starbeam, Sunshine, Raindrop. Could have been Greentea, Nettle, Strawberry, Amaryllis, Elderberry, Quince, Cobweb, Sapphire. Marshmallow or Silk, Velvet, Peace—names not found in *The Big Book of Baby*. Names, but gentler names that reflected the hopes of parents in the Swinging Sixties! Baby Saffron became Saffron through a couple of coincidental circumstances, signs from above. Her mother and I had gone through the usual arguments over names, concentrating on boys simply because the Aldridge men had failed to produce a girl in four generations. She liked Albert. Me, I chose Ruben. We both hated each other's suggestion, so when little Saffron came screaming into the world we had to rethink. Rita reminded me that I had named our first child, a boy, Miles, and this was going to be her choice—Elizabeth Rose!!! I argued against it—too upper middle class, too much like an accountant's daughter. I argued for Juliette—Juliette Gréco being a desperate passion. Rita was adamant the new baby would be Elizabeth. It would need something extraordinary to shift her opinion! The coincidence happened at my studio on Litchfield Street off Charing Cross Road. The radio was playing Donovan's new single "Mellow Yellow" as I was opening the morning's mail, the usual pile of bills and tax demands. But one envelope intrigued. It was from India, the handwriting elegant and the mushy smells it emitted, sexy. Opened the envelope, which contained an intricately folded sheet of vellum, like a tiny origami pocket, holding a single stem of a flower, like a yellow crocus. On the vellum was written simply, "Saffron is Beautiful and so are you." Nothing else. As I read the words, Donovan crooned "I'm just wild about Saffron..." It seemed a portent. The little girl would be named Saffron. Rita loved it too.

Q.E.D. Hi, Saff. Hope you like my little epistle. Love, Your Dad.

Saffron Aldridge, dressed in Chanel and green rubber wellies, stands in the archway of a stone colonnade at the end of her garden. Two small changing rooms, now used for storage, once served a swimming pool in the 1920s.

Above: Irving Penn's photograph of two stacked skulls rests on the fireplace mantle in the drawing room next to a red glass egg that Saffron found at a local junk shop. The female nude was taken by Edward Weston. Opposite: Saffron, a model for seventeen years and once the "face" of Ralph Lauren's campaign, sits on a French armchair in her drawing room. The framed poster, *Chelsea Girl* (model, Penelope Tree), was designed in 1969 by Saffron's father, famed graphic artist Alan Aldridge, for an Andy Warhol film of the same name. Next pages, left: Female head, by Alan Aldridge, 1967, its features loosely based on Saffron's mother. "I like the way the moss grows over the head; it looks like hair," says Saffron. Next pages, right: An overpowering large plaster bust of Lenin, found in a Russian art shop in Notting Hill, rests upon a simple Indian chest in the drawing room.

Who is your favorite character in history?
Elizabeth I.

Who is your favorite painter?
Francisco de Goya.

What is the quality you most admire in a man?
Fidelity.

What is the quality you most admire in a woman?
Energy.

Who would you have liked to be?
My boyfriend, so I know what he is thinking.

What is your principal defect?
Speaking before I think.

What to your mind would be the greatest of misfortunes?
Any pain to my children.

Who is your favorite hero of fiction?
The Indian Chief Bromden from *One Flew Over the Cuckoo's Nest.*

What is your favorite bird?
Tandoori chicken.

SOLINA AND NICOLAS GUÉDROÏTZ

BY THE COUNTESS OF ALBEMARLE

High ceilings, bright light, space and serene white walls are not the typical characteristics of a house in the heart of South Kensington. Nor is it a typical contemporary home based on the harsh philosophy of "less is more" with hardly any evidence of daily life.

The Guédroïtz have successfully accomplished an exercise of extremes and contrasts: modern juxtaposed with classic, contemporary with antique furniture, photography with old master paintings, silence and music, discipline and fantasy.

All these extreme elements stem, no doubt, from their diverse origins yet similar backgrounds, opposite yet complementary characters and their early passage through New York. They met at an uptown party, discovered a common passion for Russia, and when Solina decided it was time to leave, Nicolas was prompt to escort her. Their fate was sealed.

Nicolas, third generation of White Russians, is an expert and dealer in antique Russian furniture, Tula objects and books. Solina, a talented photographer of French and Italian descent, collects the Diaghilev Ballets Russes theatre designs, Soviet photography and Russian avant-garde artists. They passionately love Russian classical and modern music, and their children are raised to the sound of Shostakovich's symphonies, Stravinsky ballet music and Prokofiev's *Peter and the Wolf.*

Rarely has a house been so representative of its owners' characters and achieved at the same time a perfect balance, harmony and understanding around a common taste for what is Russian, whether old or new. With such a strong personal vision, their architect Michael Wolfson took great joy in working with them and bringing their

Solina and Nicolas Guédroïtz's drawing room. A white tiger skin from India was a gift to Nicolas's grandfather. The Russian tiger wood armchair was designed by Vassily Stasov.

concepts to life. During one of their meetings, which I happened to attend, I was thoroughly impressed by a beautiful sectional perspective model in clear acrylic and cardboard that clearly outlined the complexity of the task that lay ahead. Indeed, it was a technical and logistical challenge to combine four separate apartments and make them work together as one home. Wolfson says, "I was not the first architect to deal with this complicated project, and to see the Guédroïtz approve and understand my architectural solutions made the project even more rewarding."

The modern structure and spacious layout that they elaborated together has simply created the most perfect backdrop for their outstanding Russian furniture collection, a contrast which is again found with the Old Master paintings hanging alongside Russian propaganda, avant-garde art and photography. It all sounds so easy, but I must however emphasize that the outcome is clearly the result of patience and sacrifice during a long period of a few years, trials, errors and tribulations.

When I first met the Guédroïtz, they were living on the top and first floor, which were not directly connected, and with the main entrance in the next-door building, inevitably confusing their visitors and probably you, the reader, too. Then they moved to the ground floor, then had to retire to the

Ex Libris

432 Chaque signe, isolément, semble mort.
Qu'est-ce qui lui donne vie? Il n'est vivant que dans
l'usage. A-t-il alors un souffle de vie? Ou bien
l'usage est-il son souffle?

Previous pages, left: Nicolas handling two rare pieces, late 18th century, from the Imperial army factory of Tula: a candlestick and an incense burner. Previous pages, right: The Chinese daybed in the drawing room is flanked by two of Solina's black-and-white photographs of Stalinesque architecture of the 1950s. The portrait above is of Leopold I of Belgium.

Above, left: Nicolas stands in front of what he claims might be the first example of Russian pop art: a stamp mosaic of a Russian woman by Enko Arovsky, 1885. Above, right: Toy soldiers from the French Imperial guard are part of young Alexis Guédroïtz's collection. The soldiers stand upon a leather-bound volume of hand-colored drawings for the loggia of Raffael at the Vatican, mid-18th-century. The desk is a Russian minister's desk, dating from 1793, and the chair with sunburst motif, also Russian, 1790.

Below, left: Solina, a photographer of faces and façades, upstairs in her study reviewing her photographs for an exhibition. Below, right: On the wall above the red mantle in the drawing room are stage set and costume designs for the Ballets Russes, circa 1910. The vintage poster inside the hearth is a ballet costume design by Picasso, signed by Serge Lifar.

basement, combining this unsettling migration with the exhilaration of an expanding family and the creation of their gallery. But in the midst of this disarray, they always showed determination, an unshakable sense of humor and a unique sense of style. Solina is often seen whizzing around London in her customized Mini Morris and intrinsic Italo-French driving skills. Nicolas, variously with or without beard (a continuous source of arguments during which I have often been asked to take sides!) but always sporting impeccably cut suits, is to my knowledge one of the most elegant men I know, and the most eccentric. During the harshest times of construction work, he set up his "cafeteria" at one of the best restaurants on Pimlico Road across the road from the gallery. But in order to feel more at home, he had the table set with their own dinner service and cutlery. Solina would often join him for lunch, always radiant and eclectically chic, despite having a home in the making.

As soon as one rings the doorbell, one realizes this is no ordinary home just by noticing the modern chrome door accessories on the traditional glossy black door. As you enter, you are immediately greeted and surprised by a sense of space and light. As you are led up the sleek lime oak stairs, you get a glimpse of the library, modern in structure but clearly consisting of beautifully bound antique books, and if you can browse a little closer, you will notice the children's colorful toys and the father's toys from his childhood, consisting of antique lead soldiers displayed on the mantelpiece and the old miniature cannon.

What do you regard as the lowest depth of misery?
Misery, poverty.

Where would you like to live?
Moscow.

What is your idea of earthly happiness?
No idea.

To what fault do you feel most indulgent?
Mediocrity.

Who is your favorite hero of fiction?
The villain in *James Bond*.

Who is your favorite hero in real life?
My wife.

Who is your favorite character in history?
Stalin.

Who is your favorite painter?
Francis Bacon.

Who is your favorite musician?
Dmitry Shostakovich.

Who is your favorite writer?
Fyodor Dostoyevsky.

What is the quality you most admire in a man?
Fearlessness.

What is the quality you most admire in a woman?
Intelligence.

What is your favorite virtue?
Gratitude.

What is your favorite occupation?
Listening to live Russian modern music.

Who would you have liked to be?
Stravinsky.

What is your most marked characteristic?
Boredom during parties.

What is your principal defect?
Laziness.

What to your mind would be the greatest of misfortunes?
Missing a fortune.

What is your favorite color?
Orange.

What is your favorite bird?
The firebird.

On the first landing, after having passed by Russian propaganda art and a bust of Alexander II by an ancestral sculptor (Romuald Giedroyc), you face an airy dining room where the elements of contrast are found in the now-classic Norman Foster chrome and glass dining table and antique chairs covered in strikingly modern orange fabric, a choice I was kindly consulted upon when a decision between contemporary orange or rustic black-and-white cowhide had to be made.

You then walk up a few more stairs and, as you are flanked by an Empire console and an unusual "pre-pop art" nineteenth-century postal stamp collage, you face a large and serene reception room, where again the modern sofas designed by their architect juxtapose Russian armchairs, Nicolas's grand piano and Solina's collection of Bakst, Exter and Gontcharova watercolors. Even the curtains, modern in their simplicity, exude an old-time era in the choice of powder blue silk fabric. My favorite corner has to be the Chinese daybed, where on many occasions I have reinvented the world with Solina and told stories to her children, Alexis and Sveva, while Nicolas would treat us to a piano sonata in a cloud of cigar puffs. This is a perfect reception room to entertain friends and clients, and every July they fill it up with an open house party to celebrate Nicolas's birthday, following the vivacious summer opening reception with Russian musicians, caviar and vodka at the gallery on Pimlico Road.

The study, with its interesting and minimalist skylight, though on the next floor is a visual part of the reception room, separated only by the lime oak stairs and cutout white banister wall and by glass, through which one can notice an intricate Russian desk. I have been a fortunate guest on many occasions and have been able to see all the various parts of the house—the bedrooms, the ultramodern limestone bathrooms and the children's quarters. They all share the same qualities as the rest of the house and its philosophy, where there is no conflict in the eclectic opposites as with the owners, only harmony, and that is the result of living with passion, love, perseverance and vision. They have been married now for ten years and have dedicated, and will continue to do so, their time to lifelong projects: their house, their internationally respected and renowned gallery on Pimlico Road, their children, their collection, their love for music, and their grateful friends such as myself.

Alexis and Sveva Guédroïtz in the family library play with Alexis's toy soldiers. The austere Russian minister's desk from 1793 is offset by two contemporary red and yellow cross cushions. The 19th-century painting above the mantle is of three horsemen, one an ancestor of Nicolas's in the campaign of Schleswig Holstein. Below the canvas are three framed photographs taken by Solina, which received an award on travel photography.

INDIA JANE BIRLEY

BY MIRANDA BROOKS

All of India Jane's various homes have had some common elements: dogs of a variety of breeds, enormous amounts of dog hair, and dog beds in every room; a vast choice of teas depending on the current faze, chai from her four years in India, her current favorite Tum Song. The most familiar mark is weeks and weeks of no toilet paper and no lightbulbs, which in her present house with many floors generally means blindly feeling your way upstairs at night, and trying to put on makeup in a shadowy bathroom.

There have, however, been some changes over the years in how Jane lives, most excitingly in the kitchen. About twelve years ago, her kitchen only produced a strict color palette of white and brown: hot milk, mashed potatoes, dates and opium, and the very occasional fish pie following a recipe from Mark's, her father's club. Then came a lovely chicken with green sauce, a husband, four years in India and the necessity of teaching her cook to cook. Now, Jane's dinners in London are treats: her tablecloths ravishing and a riot of color, lovely glasses from Venice, delicious wine— thank you, Francis—and fine, delicate cooking that you pay attention to. Despite her talent, her husband has to organize dinners or he would never be fed and have to live off sprouts—Jane's favorite food; she says it's boiled eggs.

Jane rarely socializes; she has no time. The very early part of the day and often the end are spent in a form of contemplation, of an esoteric kind. Dog walks and the requirements of Nina, her queenly and vicious Indian Pie dog, and Mickey, her rescued and slightly fragile whippet, steal time away from her real pursuit, painting. Jane's pictures are populated with the inhabitants of her life, as with Vermeer. Friends appear in scene after scene. I was recently Diana the Huntress, and then a Leda-ish figure with a swan, but the swan turned back into a dog, her favorite model. Jane's portraits deepen with her feelings for the person, soften and come to life. Her landscapes, currently the beach in Deal, are

Where would you like to live?
Calcutta.

What is your idea of earthly happiness?
A small feast after a small famine.

Who are your favorite characters in history?
Florence Nightingale, Admiral Horatio Nelson,
Duke of Wellington.

Who is your favorite artist?
Johannes Vermeer.

Who is your favorite musician?
Dinu Lipatti.

Who are your favorite writers?
Joseph Conrad, Yukio Mishima, Kawabata Yasunari.

What is the quality you most admire in a man?
A flashy intellect.

What is the quality you most admire in a woman?
Wit.

What is your favorite occupation?
Painting.

Who would you have liked to be?
A set designer.

What is your most marked characteristic?
Ask any ex-boyfriend.

What do you most value in your friends?
The way they value friendship.

What is your principal defect?
A tendency to despondency.

What to your mind would be the greatest of misfortunes?
To be undone by any misfortune.

What is your favorite color?
All greens, all yellows, all blues.

What is your favorite bird?
Black-winged stilt.

really an excuse for some inner dreamlike expression. Weeks spent painting pebbles no doubt contribute to the daydream quality.

Jane is the slowest decorator ever. The house became habitable floor by floor, and about a year at a time. It's a miracle that the spare room is habitable, despite the fact that she manages to have an almost permanent guest or girlfriend in residence. India supplied some furniture, in particular a huge bed that could sleep a family of six and that she has to climb into off a chair (very princess and the pea). Francis spends most of his time in a huge fluffy white beanbag with Mickey. Her favorite possessions are her icons of St. Nicholas and St. John the Baptist. The only thing that I really covet is her signed letter from Florence Nightingale and a portrait. Everything in the house is lovely and full of character, but you would never normally think to assemble all these personalities in one room. Jane has a real talent for picture hanging—lovely compositions of Russian posters, Japanese prints, paintings of radishes, and photographs. The kitchen has such a fantastic collection of books (many of which have forbidden crisp packets hiding behind them), that you could live quite happily in it for a number of years.

With all Jane's habits, she rarely goes away. Her mother's house in Spain is one of the few places she will go, for a few days. On my first trip with her, she spent her whole time creeping from one shady spot to the next like a long pale piece of spaghetti in a huge hat, painting a very gloomy palm tree. Our one outing to the village resulted in terrible drunkenness and Jane's wrap skirt revealing her lack of knickers to the fascination of all the locals. This was nothing compared to the trip home on a very full charter flight. Jane, who insists on dressing to travel, was looking like a demented Jackie O. in high-heeled pink espadrilles stolen from her mother's cupboard, sunglasses and the huge hat again. Her drink of choice at the time was Bailey's, which she swigged from the bottle the whole way home. Her husband has gently begun to persuade her into the joys of traveling with trips to Damascus, but sunbathing and eating holidays have her heading home early and back to the studio. Since the arrival of her garden, she has begun

First page: India Jane Birley lounges on top of her dining room table. Her cherished books and a collection of photographs and prints occupy each wall. A horn chandelier with an ostrich egg finial from London dealer Adam Bray hangs above.

Previous page: A portrait by India Jane of a friend rests against a scale model of a tug on a small side table in the study.

Opposite, left: A portrait by Oswald Birley of India's aunt, Maxime de la Falaise, opposite the French Art Deco olive wood desk in the study.

Opposite, right: Mickey, a Whippett, and Nina, a mongrel, brought home from India, are India Jane's constant companions.

Right: Two framed letters written by Florence Nightingale, India Jane's heroine, rest on the mantle in the drawing room, flanked by a photograph of General Smutts and a stuffed pike India Jane gave to her husband, Francis Pike.

to conquer a lifelong fear of worms. Now she can be persuaded to clip her escallonia into a mini bonsai world and direct orders to Francis to power hose and clean. Jane controls people with a variety of tactics: cups of tea, delicacies, overt flattery, and orders like "move you fat slug." She is tyrannical while giving the appearance of helplessness. Opening letters, buying lightbulbs, getting a parking permit are beyond her. She refuses to do what bores her, and is quite happy to live with and accept the resulting disorder. There is also a strong "Jean" streak which results in outfits that she wears for months on end with horrible Birkenstocks and bathcaps in the evening—she has a collection. She also has a collection of jewelry, seldom seen due to its incompatibility with appalling scruffiness. Once in a diamond necklace, the hidden, long fingered, racy Bodacea comes out and all around her are either lashed by the wicked tongue or reduced to weeping giggles.

Jane is not straightforward. She rarely inhabits her beguiling outer form and constructs some form of web, rather to protect herself than to entrap. She does not need to entrap, as everything she does allures, from her paintings to her home and to her cooking. She has a constant assurance that this is how things should be done, particularly concerning diet—her husband being her guinea pig for each new approach. Her bathroom shelves are heaving under evidence of a multitude of new approaches, as various treatments and creams have been embarked on and abandoned for something better, all with complete faith. Her interests move with a similar pace and involvement: dousing, automatic writing, Christianity, making her own pigments, baroque music—not that "horrible modern stuff"—and *always* on vinyl, herbal remedies, homeopathy, politics, Jung. Never a dull moment. Most around her find there is no point in trying to keep pace with these mental meanderings, as they follow such an idiosyncratic and invisible map.

KATE REARDON

BY GRAYDON CARTER

It all began with Taki. Like Vikings who brought home word of the New World, he was the first to publicly herald in his column in *The Spectator* in the late eighties Kate Reardon—English rose with the freshness of a dewy meadow. She was a slip of a girl then, with straight blond hair, eyes the color of the vault of heaven, skin that possessed the luster of a china tea cup, and she was just this side of 20. Minus the just-this-side-of-twenty part, she's still all that.

When Taki "discovered" her, Kate was working as a fashion assistant to Elizabeth Saltzman at American *Vogue*. "I would go on sittings and forget the shoes," she says. "We'd be on a shoot four hours outside of New York, with helicopters flying people in and vans and clothes everywhere, and we would have to crop all the photographs off at the knees. I was the *Guinness Book of World Records* worst fashion assistant." She stayed two years and then returned to England. "It was my first job. My first paycheck. And I returned home a virgin."

After eight years as the fashion editor at *Tatler*, she began writing more and came to work for me at *Vanity Fair*.

She lives in South Kensington and in a cottage in Wiltshire, three miles from Stonehenge. (If you're on the A303 and you hear a woman whizzing down the highway in a beat-up Golf singing Neil Diamond's "Sweet Caroline" at the top of her lungs, well, that's Kate. "When it comes to music, it's anything I can dance to. In that respect, I'm a complete tart.")

The last time I saw her was at a garden party in London. Kate's then-boyfriend was working and she dragged me along as her date. We were making our way through the crowd and bumped into Taki. He appeared to flush a bit when he saw Kate. And who could blame him?

BY VASSI CHAMBERLAIN

Should Kate Reardon ever invite you to visit her at what she calls her "penthouse in South Kensington," there are certain things you should know. The most important is that she does not live in

Previous page: English rose Kate Reardon in her drawing room below a translucent antelope lantern.
Above, left: White letters "K, A, T, E" found at local junk shops sit among Kate's books on fashion and style on a drawing room shelf.
Above, right: A bulletin board in Kate's kitchen filled with invitations, the most prized an invitation from Queen Elizabeth II to mark the decade birthdays of the Queen Mother (100), Princess Margaret (70), Princess Anne (50) and Prince Andrew (40).
Below, left: Two riding crops, once belonging to Kate's grandfather, lie on a side table in front of a sculpture of a woman's breasts by Kate Braine. The charcoal drawing of horses is by A. Munnings.
Below, right: Kate at her dressing table in a Chanel coat. The roses are from her garden in Wiltshire.

salubrious South Kensington, but above the Gloucester Road branch of Burger King. You should also know that she will expect you to arrive on time, which, given her reluctance to tell you exactly where she lives, is unlikely, particularly as you will have had to walk up five floors and will have endured a few tense moments explaining your tardiness. When your breathing has returned to normal, you will notice that her "penthouse" displays evidence of the obsessive-compulsive. Kate abhors untidiness and guests are often encouraged to plump up cushions. It is, therefore, a tribute to her considerable charms that so many of us visit her quite so often. Her misplaced sense of reality is perhaps due to the fact she was absurdly old moving out of home, although she did make a bid for freedom at 19 by moving to New York to work for American *Vogue*. She was soon back in the family bosom when, at 21, she accepted the post of fashion editor of *Tatler*. She remained there as fashion director for seven years. Having "grown out" of fashion, the former *Times* columnist is now a full-time writer. She celebrated her first literary triumph at the age of six when she won a Cindy's World from the back of a cornflakes box by completing the sentence "I love Cindy because..." She did somewhat presciently with the words: "Because she does everything I want to do when I grow up." This must have included owning a cottage in the country. An invitation to her rose-covered hideaway in Wiltshire is highly prized. Her application to tidiness is a small price to pay, for once the rules are understood, the entire weekend is spent in pajamas, disturbed only by visits to the pub or spots of topless badminton, to the great but delighted surprise of the local squire, who once dropped by unannounced to deliver a trout. Kate has exquisite taste. And, like her cottage, she decorated the London flat herself, making the curtains on a twenty-year-old sewing machine, the very one on which she made her first ballgown. It now vibrates like Mount Vesuvius. When she first bought the flat, she thought: "I want an all-white modern apartment," but knew that she would be suicidal within hours and that no one would ever visit her. She compromised with cream and beige. She is now only half suicidal, and well we already know about the problem she has with visitors.

So what else is odd about Kate? Recent favorite birthday presents include a cordless power drill and a set of screwdrivers. She eats two chocolate bars a day, loves Neil Diamond and refuses to ever go skiing. And her friends are particularly fond of the stiff-upper-lip-style aphorisms that she often comes out with. One last word of warning: don't ever let her get her hands on a bottle of Cuervo Gold; her sweet nature will instantly evaporate. She will make you play board games until you beg her to stop, then she will humiliate you over a round of spin the bottle. Other than that, she makes an uncommonly perfect friend.

What do you regard as the lowest depth of misery?
Bereavement.

What is your idea of earthly happiness?
Requited love.

To what faults do you feel most indulgent?
Sanctimony, laziness and overanalysis.

Who is your favorite character in history?
Henry VIII—I've got a bit of a crush.

Who is your favorite artist?
Nic Fiddian-Green. I long for one of his monumental horse heads.

Who is your favorite writer?
William Blake.

What is the quality you most admire in a man?
An ability to appreciate that I'm doing him the most enormous favor.

What is your favorite virtue?
Kindness.

What is your favorite occupation?
Laughing.

Who would you have liked to be?
It would be rude to my parents to want to be anyone else.

JEMMA KIDD

BY GEORGE LAZENBY

Jemma is an extraordinarily relaxed busy person, always running around London at 150 miles per hour. For a true homebody, she is a constant traveler. She likes nothing better than staying home, a place that is her sanctuary. It is quite a comfortable, cozy, nest-like environment. She has surrounded herself with calming influences, such as fresh flowers, crystals, tuberose and jasmine candles, to escape the hectic lifestyle she leaves at the front door. There is, however, a constant flow of every magazine under the sun—a necessary evil of work to stay always ahead of the trends since, in her profession as a makeup artist, they are constantly evolving. Much of what is in her house is deliberately reminiscent of her spiritual home in Barbados, the island on which she spent her happiest childhood years. She always has plants such as palm trees to keep her fondest memories of her distant Caribbean home alive. The most noticeable thing of all are the hundreds of framed photographs of family and friends on every surface, proof of her first priority in life: her loved ones.

If you open the kitchen cupboards or refrigerator, you will only find the healthiest organic foods, as she loves to go to the markets for the freshest of goods, evidence of her personal credo "You are what you eat." She is a firm believer in healthy body, healthy mind. Special Chinese cleansing teas are always in abundance; the kettle is permanently at a boil.

The most overwhelming room in her house is her bathroom, which is like walking into a chemist or Harvey Nichols's beauty hall. Her work in the beauty and makeup industry has created somewhat of an addiction to products of every size, shape and price. No price range has been left unexplored. Everything must

London "It" girl Jemma Kidd on her silver Piaggio Vespa, "the only way to get around town."

be thoroughly investigated firsthand. She has every brush, cream, cleanser and powder known to man, and has a use for every single one. A virtual makeup mountain!! Her flatmate is forever assisting in her research (and loving it). She loves nothing better than luring friends into the "makeup cave" to give them makeovers, whether they're willing or not. And no one escapes without having had a proper eyebrow tweeze. Anytime, any age, any place, she doesn't even go to the shops without some form of beauty aid tucked up her sleeve. The next fashion emergency could be right around the corner.

As one walks through the front door one nearly falls over the massive amounts of gum boots, riding hats and polo sticks, as horses are in her blood. A former member of the Junior British dressage team, her motto has recently become "If you can't beat 'em, join 'em," since her father, brother and sister are all professional polo players. Her weekend lessons have begun, and the bruises from her latest passion are visible everywhere, caused by the family battles on the polo pitch. Whenever she has a spare weekend, she is back in the countryside getting her share of dirt under her fingernails. Plus, she can't keep herself away from her brother's first child, baby Jaden.

Aside from the calm feeling of Jemma's home, her hectic life is inescapable, and the phone rings constantly. Friends, family and business contacts have to fight to get through on her constantly engaged cell phone, but she always has time for everyone. No matter how far her travels for work or pleasure take her, everyone knows she is always available, no matter how trivial or unimportant the call may seem.

If one asks anyone who knows Jemma, they will say one of her most marked characteristics is her intuitive ability to know what to say in any situation. No one has an unkind word about her. She is nearly as professional in her work as she is professional as a party-goer.

What do you regard as the lowest depth of misery?
Incurable illness.

Where would you like to live?
England.

What is your idea of earthly happiness?
Being surrounded by my loved ones
on a Caribbean island.

To what faults do you feel most indulgent?
No self-discipline.

Who is your favorite hero of fiction?
James Bond.

Who are your favorite heroes in real life?
Aid workers; my mother.

Who is your favorite character in history?
Elizabeth I.

Who is your favorite painter?
Claude Monet.

Who is your favorite musician?
Bob Marley.

Who is your favorite writer?
J.R.R. Tolkien.

What is the quality you most admire in a man?
Humor, kindness, unselfishness, manners.

What is the quality you most admire in a woman?
Loyalty, sincerity, honesty.

What is your favorite virtue?
Unconditional love.

What is your favorite occupation?
Horse riding.

Who would you have liked to be?
Madonna for a day.

What is your most marked characteristic?
Nonjudgmental.

What do you most value in your friends?
Support, fun, loyalty.

What is your principal defect?
Nonconfrontational.

*What to your mind would be the greatest
of misfortunes?*
To live longer than my children.

What is your favorite color?
Turquoise.

What is your favorite bird?
Flamingo.

Previous page: Jemma plays with her Jack Russell, Circus, in the drawing room of the family townhouse she shares with her brother Jack Kidd (a professional polo player), his wife, Catherine, and their daughter, Jaden. Catherine and Jack found the sailboat at Bermondsey market in London. The mantle is lined with miniature Tibetan Buddhas and a small watercolor of the seaside view in front of the Kidd's family house in Barbados. The oil painting of the child asleep in the chair belonged to Catherine's grandmother.

Above: Jemma, her brother Jack and Jaden. The walnut cabinet from the Newark outdoor antique market houses many of Jack's silver polo trophies, cups and ribbons and serves as a place to hang his polo mallets.

Left: Jemma in the kitchen leans alongside a bronze horse won by Jack in a polo tournament in Spain.

DETMAR BLOW

BY ARTHUR HAMILTON

Questioned recently in Los Angeles by a puzzled gallerist who did not understand his role in the Modern Art gallery of which he is a director, Detmar replied that it was simple. He made the tea.

Detmar Blow was born in Stroud, a former textile town in Gloucestershire. He grew up with his brother, Amaury, and sister, Selina, at Hilles, an Arts and Crafts house with a view overlooking five counties built by his namesake architect grandfather, who had been discovered in Normandy at age 19 by John Ruskin while on a traveling scholarship from the South Kensington Schools of Art. Detmar's grandfather went on to organize the burial of William Morris and had one of the most successful architectural practices in London at the turn of the twentieth century. Hilles had an artistic, bohemian environment. Detmar's German great-grandmother had been taught the piano by Clara Schumann and learned to speak Italian with Mrs. Oscar Wilde. Detmar's father had been a writer who, in Berlin in 1945, interrogated Hannah Reitsch, the last person to see Hitler alive, and afterwards had worked under Ian Fleming as a foreign and diplomatic correspondent for the Kemsley newspapers. He met Detmar's mother, a beautiful Sri Lankan–born Worth model, at a fashion show. Later they married, he 42 years old to her 17. After Detmar's father died, when he was 14, the family went to live for part of the year in Sri Lanka. Detmar's Sri Lankan grandmother had gone to the Slade School of Art in the 1930s, and his great-aunt Minnette de Silva was a pupil and perhaps lover of Le Corbusier, or "Corb" as she referred to him. She later pioneered modernist architecture with traditional materials in South Asia.

His Sri Lankan grandfather owned a tiny island, Taprobane, 100 yards off the southern tip of the main island, which was then rented by Stash Klossowski, the elder son of Balthus. The house, built in the 1930s by Count de Mauny, was shaped like a star, and from the central lotus hall the sea is visible from each side. The gardens, designed by De Mauny and his boyfriend Rahman, were inspired by the Vatican gardens. A fusion of cultures from east and west is the essence of Detmar's background. In August at the end of monsoon season, Detmar worked on the house, painting the cadjan shutters. When marooned on the island, he learned to cook curries and to add brown sugar to the curry to reduce the heat from adding too much chili powder. He learned to use the telephone in Sri Lanka, and as Stash Klossowski pointed out, like John Lennon, Detmar never redialed when the phone line was engaged. When Detmar was 16, his mother and his siblings went to Las Vegas, where his mother remarried at the Little Church of the West. After the ceremony, they went to Ceasar's Palace to a concert given by Frank Sinatra whose autograph Detmar acquired backstage for his sister.

Detmar went to the LSE where he read history, studying the Middle East in the time of the Crusades, eighteenth-century architecture and furniture, the Tudors with David Starkey, and the Lyons silk industry. He

Detmar Blow seated in the stairwell of his flat in Waterloo. The yellow floor painted throughout by artist Richard Woods, entitled "Rustic daisy repeat." Above the staircase hang black-and-white photographs of Andy Warhol by Alistair Thain. Over the door frame, a photograph by Arnaud Bani of Detmar wearing Christian Dior haute couture and a top hat designed by Detmar's friend Philip Treacy.

Above: Detmar and Issie Blow's dining room with a laminated aluminum cardboard table and chairs designed by David Bartlett. The fountain on the wall, by artists Sue Webster and Tim Noble, is entitled "Excessive sensual indulgence." Below: In the dining room, a Sean Ellis photograph of Honor Fraser, framed by Colin Glen. The two cans above are baked bean tins entitled "British rubbish," by artists Sue Webster and Tim Noble. Opposite: A series of photographs on the wall by Sean Ellis and styled by Detmar's wife, Issie Blow, feature Erin O'Connor for a story for *The Face* magazine. Above the fireplace is a sculpture by Ian Dawson. A leather Asprey trunk filled with Issie's clothes lies open next to a sculpture called "Eternal Love" by Colin Glen, depicting the story line for a movie, *White Mischief*, based on Detmar's grandparents.

What do you regard as the lowest depth of misery?
No cigars.

Where would you like to live?
In an ivory tower.

What is your idea of earthly happiness?
Breakfast in Sri Lanka.

To what faults do you feel most indulgent?
Clothes. I love flamboyant clothes.

Who are your favorite heroes of fiction?
Dracula, because he has style and girls; Pierre
Bezuhov from *War and Peace*, a conscientious
pacifist who goes off to fight the French with a
brolly; and Becky Sharp in *Vanity Fair* because
she's a scheming bitch.

Who are your favorite heroes in real life?
The Sex Pistols, I love their sense of freedom;
Margaret Thatcher, because she taught people
to work again; and my darling wife, Issie Blow,
who's a combination of the two.

Who are your favorite characters in history?
Napoléon's Foreign Minister, Charles Maurice
de Talleyrand—an elegant rebel with a great
sense of humor. Napoléon referred to him as
"shit in a silk stocking." The revolutionary
Comte de Mirabeau said of him, "He would
exchange his soul for a pile of dung, and he'd
be right to do so." Sitting Bull, who was a Teton
Dakota Indian chief, because he was fighting
for his liberty against overwhelming odds—a
dignified man with a rare respect for nature.

Who is your favorite painter?
Piero della Francesca. His paintings are a great
inspiration to me. His light and his sense of
color are so chic.

Who is your favorite musician?
Bryan Ferry. He makes such ethereal music.
It's as romantic as it is timeless.

Who is your favorite writer?
Irvine Welsh, who writes with great honesty
and humor.

What is the quality you most admire in a man?
Balls.

What is the quality you most admire in a woman?
Tits.

What is your favorite virtue?
Vice.

What is your favorite occupation?
I love working in my gallery Modern Art,
73 Redchurch Street, Shoreditch, London.

Who would you have liked to be?
François-Auguste-René de Chateaubriand.
By the time he was 21, he'd gone to Versailles,
been kicked out of France, fought against the
revolutionaries, hung out with Iroquois Indians
and met George Washington. He was a fearless
man with a great love of women.

What is your most marked characteristic?
My voice.

What do you most value in your friends?
Humor, loyalty and credit cards that
actually work.

What is your principal defect?
My past.

*What to your mind would be the greatest
of misfortunes?*
Having to be thrifty.

What is your favorite color?
Pink.

What is your favorite bird?
Nightingale.

Opposite, left: Detmar enjoys the fleeting rays of sunshine in his garden designed by Tommaso del Buono.
Opposite, right: Two Native American Indian dolls by artist Brad Kahlhamer in Detmar's garden.

spent his time with Lebanese, Spanish and South Americans and particularly enjoyed the excitement of Greek and Jewish parties and dancing in a Zorba-like frenzy. After LSE, Detmar qualified as a barrister. His Sri Lankan grandfather had defended 3,000 murder cases in that country, and his mother's brother, Desmond, was an eminent QC in England. At the same time, he was obliged to return to Gloucestershire, where he had inherited some property and to deal with ten years of unpaid taxes and debts from his mother's Las Vegas marriage.

Detmar was not to spend long in Gloucestershire. In 1988, at a wedding at Salisbury Cathedral, a dynamic, driven and restless force entered Detmar's life: Isabella Delves Broughton. Isabella wore an ostrich feather hat, a purple Rifat Ozbek coat with matching purple Manolo Blahnik shoes. He was in his maternal grandfather's ambassadorial coat. They became engaged to be married sixteen days later and married at Gloucester Cathedral the following year. Isabella immediately insisted that Detmar return to London and practice as a barrister. For six long years, Detmar traveled from the Temple to courts in London and the southeast of England, fighting divorce and criminal cases. Back at their then London home, 67 Elizabeth Street, Belgravia, Isabella had installed her fashion causes: Philip Treacy and Alexander McQueen. To counterbalance the sudden abundance of high fashion in his life, Detmar allowed his Persian friend Amir Farman Farma—who was doing a Ph.D. at Oxford—to complete it with them in London. Away from academic study, Amir's amorous involvements included Madonna and Uma Thurman. Art was not totally absent from Detmar's life; evenings after court would be spent with his friend James Birch, who was curating exhibitions of Francis Bacon in Moscow and Gilbert & George in Peking.

A decade later, in February 1998, Detmar met Stuart Shave at a dinner at the Metropolitan Hotel that Isabella and David LaChapelle were having to celebrate the end of a photo shoot at an old asylum near Heathrow airport with the models Sophie Dahl and Devon. Stuart, aged 23, was assisting Isabella. Detmar and Stuart got talking, so much so that they actually missed a chance to meet Madonna. In November 1998, Detmar Blow and Stuart Shave joined forces to open Modern Art gallery at 73 Redchurch Street, Shoreditch. The gallery was designed by Adjaye-Russell and opened with the exhibition "WOW" by Tim Noble and Sue Webster. Modern Art has made an important contribution to the London art scene with a series of dynamic shows and memorable openings, by Dinos and Jake Chapman, Brad Kahlhamer, Clare Woods, Tim and Sue, and Juergen Teller, attended by the writer and curator Gregor Muir. Modern Art is now firmly on the map as one of London's leading contemporary art galleries. Detmar lives happily with art and fashion.

CHARLOTTE STOCKDALE

BY JOSH VAN GELDER

Excerpt from "Redactrice! The lives and loves of a super-stylist"
(with apologies to Jackie Collins)

As the 747 prepared for touchdown, the steward paused for a moment before waking the radiant figure that slumbered before him. How does she do it? he thought in amazement. Only three hours of sleep and still she looks so impossibly glamorous. Perhaps it was the lustrous waves of ebony hair that framed the soft romance of her face, or the seemingly endless legs curled under the quilted cashmere blanket, designed especially for her by Hermès. Perhaps it was the fact that her feet remained daintily clad in Christian Louboutin heels while others chose to spend the flight in terry toweling sockettes. Whatever it was, one thing was for sure. If there was ever such a thing as true style, Charlotte Stockdale had it. And more.

Twenty minutes later, reclining in the back of a black cab, Charlotte smiled to herself. Thank God she was home. Much as she loved the excitement and stimulation of the catwalk shows in Paris, Milan and New York, she was always glad to return to her beloved London. Ignoring the constant buzzing of her voice mail, she picked up her cell phone and made the most important call of the day.

"Mummy? I'm home."

Charlotte's closeness to her family had always been a source of deep inner strength. Despite their aristocratic titles, Sir Thomas and his wife, Lady Stockdale, were hardly stuffy, old-fashioned parents. Tommy, both baronet and barrister, was the backbone of the British legal system. With a lineage dating back to the eleventh century and his position as Prime Warden of the Fishmongers' Guild, he was, by all accounts, a model member of the ruling classes. Only the twinkle of mischief in his eyes betrayed the fact that he was more than happy to flaunt convention, living life by his own rules.

Famed fashion stylist Charlotte Stockdale in her library wearing a secondhand dress from Steinberg and Tolken and ice skate shoes by Boudicca.

Jackie, his impossibly chic wife, was a delicate and exquisite mix of the Vietnamese and Parisian beaux mondes. While her peers were constricted by buttoned-up couture, Jackie's innate elegance allowed her to take a thrift shop T-shirt and wear it with such carefree sophistication that it out-Coco-ed Chanel. But this was no mere clotheshorse. Beneath Jackie's svelte blonde frame stood the strength of will and depth of character of a woman who had lived life to the full. Any woman who could survive the twin perils of war-torn Vietnam and the English aristocracy had strength indeed.

Having arranged dinner at the family estate in Hampshire, Charlotte had hardly put down the phone before its familiar ring started demanding her attention again. Who could it be this time? *Harper's Bazaar* calling with another job? Domenico or Stefano dialing directly from Dolce & Gabbana about the new collection? Or Camilla Lowther, the flame-haired superagent who had played a vital part in defining Charlotte's current role as one of the world's leading tastemakers? Or was it Madonna, again? Before she could even say a word in greeting, a familiar voice purred in her ear.

"I'm expecting you home in fifteen minutes. I'm wearing nothing but a bottle of champagne and a smile..."

Two hours later, as she swigged the last drops of Moët directly from the bottle, Charlotte looked down on the supine figure of her lover. Phil Poynter might be the most promising fashion photographer of his generation, she mused, but in these postcoital moments he looked like nothing more than a little boy. Phil had been a key figure in the cult that was "Cool Britannia" and in the reinvention of London as a capital of cutting-edge art and street style. He was her collaborator, her partner in crime. And a great lover, too.

He was certainly not the first. Charlotte was an intensely sexual creature, with a list of "admirers" that sounded like a selection from *Vanity Fair*'s Hot 100: the cutting-edge male supermodel, the internationally acclaimed furniture designer, the beautiful boy destined to inherit half of Scotland. She smiled fondly as she recalled them all.

But this was no time to linger in the past. She had work to do. Slipping into a pair of low-rise Luella leather hipsters and a vintage Chanel jacket, she paused to consider her options. Should she take the Mini, still festooned with stickers from the all-woman rally across the Alps? Or the Rolls Royce? No, it was still being customized by a selection of the world's finest graffiti artists, flown in from New York. No matter, the Land Rover would suit her mood better. Few would dare challenge a beautiful woman in an armored car.

Blowing her lover a farewell kiss, she headed out of the massive Hoxton loft space, pausing only to admire the two Sam Taylor-Wood photomontages that hung proudly on the wall. One featured her close friends Josh van Gelder and Katie Grand sprawled naked at an East London orgy, as an impassive Nick Cave looked on. The other showed herself and her mother in a scene of aristocratic debauchery. Nowadays, it was a rare occurrence for Charlotte to have her photograph taken. Despite her past as an internationally lauded model, she usually felt more comfortable behind the camera, using her skills as art director and stylist to create some of the most provocative images published today.

Expertly maneuvering the car through London's traffic (those years in Paris had certainly taught her the benefits of assertive driving), Charlotte reached her Pimlico home in record time. The five-story Georgian house had something of a checkered history. In a previous incarnation, it had been the secret

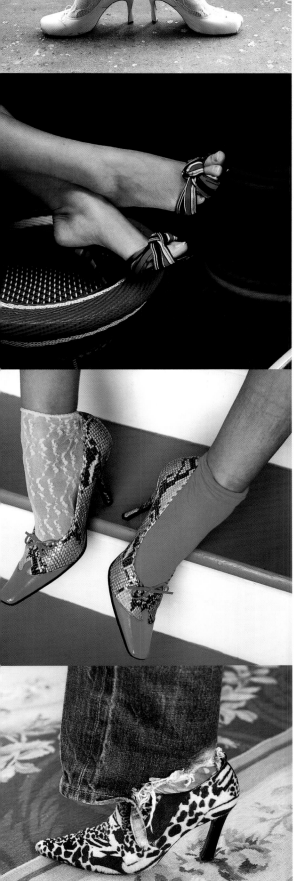

Where would you like to live?
Scotland in constant summer.

What is your idea of earthly happiness?
A self-perpetuating wine cellar.

To what faults do you feel most indulgent?
Vintage wine and shoes.

Who are your favorite heroes of fiction?
Richard Sharpe and Ripley in *Aliens*.

Who are your favorite heroes in real life?
Princess Anne and Diana Vreeland.

Who are your favorite characters in history?
Charles II and Queen Christina of Sweden.

Who is your favorite painter?
Sir Anthony Van Dyck.

Who is your favorite musician?
Sergey Rachmaninoff.

Who is your favorite writer?
Alexandre Dumas.

Who would you have liked to be?
D'Artagnan.

What is the quality you most admire in a man?
Conviction.

What is the quality you most admire in a woman?
Sense of humor.

What are your most marked characteristics?
Insouciance and a dirty laugh.

What do you most value in your friends?
The ability to enjoy themselves in any place I present them with.

What is your principal defect?
Not knowing when to stop.

What to your mind would be the greatest of misfortunes?
Being considered fashionable.

What is your favorite color?
Red.

hideaway of one of London society's most notorious womanizers. Many an indiscretion had taken place within these walls. Charlotte had torn out the ten-man Jacuzzi and the two-person power-shower (with dimmer switch) and had transformed the space into an eclectic mix of English country house style and cosmopolitan modernity. From the exquisite hand-painted wallpaper, commissioned from De Gournay that lit up her bedroom to the fluorescent pink interiors of the thirty closet doors that lined her dressing room, the house was an absolute reflection of Charlotte's personal style. Transforming the traditions of her very English background by taking them to a new, unexpected level, she created a perfect collision of Old Guard and avant-garde.

Downstairs, her office was a hive of high-fashion activity. Emily and Shirley, her two assistants were, a formidable team. Not only faultlessly efficient and endlessly creative, they also looked much better than most of the models they found themselves working with. Emily was a naturally chic, willowy blonde, whose years in New York had provided her with an effortless urban edge. Shirley was the quintessentially cool club chick, whose East London street style managed to be both sassy and classy at the same time. Charlotte strode over to her desk, waved through the conservatory windows to her landscape gardener (Nicholas, the Patagonian model that she met during the last Milan collections, who was now remodeling her home's exterior space), and launched into the day's work.

She was finalizing the plans for her latest party, taking place this weekend at the family's fourteen-bedroom home, Hoddington. Her daredevil brother John had taken time out from his busy schedule of death-defying adventures (crossing the Sahara on his turquoise Harley-Davidson, a solo trip sailing down the Amazon), to redesign and decorate the seventeenth-century mansion. He had triumphantly embraced a "Gothic Luxe" feel, with stone figurines salvaged from the moat haunting the reception rooms and a selection of medieval tapestries and weapons adding a heady ambiance. There was still much to decide. Which candelabras should be taken out for the fifty-five person seated picnic in the bluebell woods? Should she seat the *Vogue* cover girl next to the son of the Austrian Empress on Saturday or Sunday night? There were even a few close friends who had yet to respond to her invitation. She should confirm that they were definitely coming.

Charlotte picked up the phone and dialed a number from memory.

"Darling? Get me Mario Testino."

Charlotte, in her Diana Vreeland-inspired red closet, wears an Yves Saint Laurent top and knickers by Luella Bartley.

Charlotte in a Marni silk top, in the drawing room sits astride the arm of an antique leather French library club chair.

SAFFRON RAINEY ESQ.

BY RITA KONIG

Saffron was born under a lucky star, the sort that issued him an "access all areas" pass and a bucket of style. He was brought up in Wales where, as far as I can see, he and his siblings roamed free. At the age of 10, he and his brother, Gawain, bought a Mini Cooper off a local hippy who couldn't get it passed the MOT. They sped around the hills in it until one tragic day when it got smashed and even Gawain and Saffron couldn't get it past first gear.

Whenever I think of Saffron as a kid, being supremely cool with his little car, I can only imagine him like a mini-me version of how he is now, rather than as a child. His middle name is Neon, the Rolling Stones wrote a song about his mum, and it seems that all his godparents have truly fabulous and extraordinary properties around the world and no children of their own and they all adore Saffron, who is often disappearing off to a fabulous house in Morocco or inviting people to shoot at one of the best shoots in Scotland in one of the most beautiful castles. In this area, he is blessed with his "AAA" pass that that star issued him. The pass also covers London, where he is better connected than Tony Blair and certainly better dressed.

Saffron is the only boy I know who has a healthy "girl style" shoe thing going on—they are never ordinary and they are usually two-tone. But this is not to say that he is not just as happy in jeans and sneakers. Just don't expect the sneakers to be anything that you've seen advertised.

He is a modern dandy. And with so few around that really know what they are up to when it comes to getting dressed, he is the perfect sofa candy in any club, bar or house.

Saffron Rainey Esq., a statuesque 6′ 4″, on his loft-like bed, lies above his built-in miniature closet.

What do you regard as the lowest depth of misery?
Self-pity.

Where would you like to live?
A green valley in north Wales; London; Castille.

What is your idea of earthly happiness?
To love and be loved.

To what fault do you feel most indulgent?
Vanity.

Who are your favorite heroes of fiction?
Huckleberry Finn, Don Quixote, Philip Marlow, Captain Haddock.

Opposite: In the drawing room, Saffron's beloved record player sits on the Welsh flag, depicting the mythical Welsh dragon rampant on the green of the Welsh hills. The painting of the cross is a gift from Saffron's godfather and painted by Keith Millow, circa 1975. Hundreds of original 7" singles from Saffron's DJ days: soul, jazz and country favorite Bob Wills and the Texas Playboys.
Below: On top of the bedroom bureau is a painting of Saffron as a boy in the sea near Positano, Italy, by New Zealand artist Peter Thompson. Saffron's dog, Liffey (seen in the photograph by Jake Gavin) was bought from a gypsy at the Smithfield horse fair in Dublin.
Next page: Saffron and his fiancée, Cynthia Ryan, in the Art Deco entrance to the ballroom of the Park Lane Hotel in London, built between 1924 and 1927. The hotel's ballroom is referred to as London's monument to Art Deco.

Who are your favorite heroes in real life?
Jesus Christ, Wellington, Kenny Dalgliesh, George Jones.

Who are your favorite painters?
El Greco, Mike Andrews.

Who is your favorite musician?
Hank Williams.

What is the quality you most admire in a man?
Courage.

What is the quality you most admire in a woman?
Grace.

What is your favorite occupation?
Politics.

Who would you have liked to be?
Isembard Kingdom Brunel.

What do you most value in your friends?
Thoughtfulness.

What is your principal defect?
Dreaming.

What to your mind would be the greatest of misfortunes?
To value anything above love.

What is your favorite color?
The color of beach leaves in May.

What is your favorite bird?
A thrush.

TANIA BRYER
MOUFARRIGE

BY HRH PRINCESS GHIDA TALAL OF JORDAN

Walking on the cobbled streets outside Georgetown University's prestigious School of Foreign Service in Washington, D.C., it is hard not to spot a group of admirers vying for the attention of the tall blonde girl with a pronounced English accent and incessant laughter. It is the first day of school and, in the space of a few hours, the eighteen-year-old Tania Bryer has already conquered anyone who crosses her path with her million-dollar smile and unique ability to radiate warmth while relentlessly outwitting her audience.

Fast-forward ten years. A frantic Tania is waking me up at 5:25 A.M., ordering me to turn my television on as she makes her debut as Sky News' new weather girl. I watch it and doze back to sleep, only to be awakened five minutes later by an exhilarated Tania screaming: "So, how was I?" She had stumbled on her words a little and waved her hands somewhat nervously across the screen, but was determined to succeed in the cutthroat world of television. For the next two years, Tania left her mews house every morning at 4 A.M., only to return shattered every afternoon. The ubiquitous party girl surprised her detractors with an unfailing dedication to her work and succeeded in having her television show beamed by satellite across Europe and much of the world. Tania's career was always her priority. She inherited those hard-working ethics and exhilarating energy from her family. Her maternal grandmother was a pioneer as the owner of the first modeling agency in Boston. Her parents Joy and Lionel—a Rhodes scholar—added an important artistic dimension by founding and passionatley running the European Youth Orchestra, which earned her mother a Légion d'Honneur from France.

What is Tania's secret? Why is she billed as the great survivor and why do the most acerbic press commentators love her? The answer resides in the fact that Tania's warmth and empathy extend to one

Cues for TV broadcaster Tania Bryer on location at the BBC center in Shepherd's Bush.

Where would you like to live?
The Royal Suite at the Lanesborough.

What is your idea of earthly happiness?
Relaxing on a beach with my two daughters
and husband!

To what faults do you feel most indulgent?
Chocolate!!

Who are your favorite heroes of fiction?
Hagrid from *Harry Potter*, and the character
Mary from Clare Boothe Luce play and film
The Women.

Who are your favorite heroes in real life?
My parents and Nelson Mandela.

Who are your favorite characters in history?
Ghandi and Golda Meir.

Who is your favorite painter?
Andy Warhol.

What is the quality you most admire in a man?
Loyalty.

What is the quality you most admire in a woman?
Humility.

What are your favorite virtues?
Generosity and honesty.

What is your favorite occupation?
Balancing motherhood, work and being a wife!

Who would you have liked to be?
Audrey Hepburn!

What is your most marked characteristic?
My friends call me "Chatty"!

What do you most value in your friends?
Support and humor.

*What to your mind would be the greatest of
misfortunes?*
Not being healthy.

and all. She is refreshingly genuine and refuses to take herself seriously, engaging high-society priestesses and small shopkeepers with the same level of interest and concern. If one was to sum up Tania's magical potion, it would have to be that her public persona is identical to her private one: the smile does not make its appearance for the photo opportunity, and insincere comments are never offered. This down-to-earth attitude reflects itself in the unpretentious but stylish home that she has made for her family—her sports management husband, Tim, and her beautiful two daughters, Natasha Joy and newly born Francesca Lauren. Photographs of her family and friends adorn mantelpieces and walls and mingle with artifacts brought back by Tania and Tim from their various forays into Africa. In her private abode, you enter Tania's dressing area at your own peril. You would be forgiven for mistaking it for a hurricane zone: piles of dresses, trousers and shirts from the various fashion shoots lie hopelessly on the floor as the bulging closets beg for a reprieve. Magazines stacked as high as the Empire State Building are offset by the endearing sight of the myriad of stuffed animals that Tania greets every time she enters the bedroom. Monkeys and teddy bears in all shapes and sizes that have kept each other company since the carefree Georgetown days remind you that their high-flying owner has retained the youthful innocence that makes her so appealing to her friends and so disarming to her critics. The sunshine girl has not limited herself to the world of show business and Hollywood stars. She has espoused the causes of AIDS and substance abuse with relentless passion and enthusiasm. Her interest was sparked by a close friend of hers succumbing to disease. Since then, she has exerted all her energies in support of these causes. Having said all that, there is one exception when Tania will put a sudden halt to any activity she is engaged in, big or small: a desperate plea from a friend needing a sample of her never-ending positive energy. I certainly know how often I have made that call, only to feel rejuvenated in a matter of seconds: this is the Tania effect for you…

Above: Tania holding 8-week-old Francesca Lauren in the pink nursery. Framed behind the teddy bears is Tania on the cover of *OK!* magazine, celebrating the birth of her first daughter, Natasha Joy Moufarrige.

Far left: The wall of the downstairs playroom is papered with a map of the world. The arrows indicate all the places to which young Natasha Joy has traveled.

Left: Tania in her drawing room dressed in Armani. The bowls in the foreground are wedding presents from Cary and Roz Packer and Princess Ghida of Jordan.

THE WORLD

NIKKI TIBBLES

BY MARTYN THOMPSON

Nikki Tibbles is a florist with green fingers stretching from her base in W11, all over London. "No" is not the desired response to any request made by Nikki Tibbles. When a negative response is forthcoming, there is, for a brief moment, a slight furrowing of Nikki's brow. She stares quizzically, for a moment not quite believing what she is hearing. Could that have been "No," "Nada," "Non," "not possible"? Surely not.

Then, in a flash, her trademark childlike exuberance returns, and she repeats the request, this time with utter bright-eyed conviction. Ultimately, and always, that "no" becomes a "yes." Well, that's my experience, one I can attest to, since I have already photographed one flower book with the Tibs and am in the midst of book two. Nikki Tibbles is nothing if not dogged in her determination to make life bend to her way of seeing it.

That achieved, Miss Tibbles will move on to her next task. Whether that's negotiating a contract with the latest, coolest hotelier or fashion designer, or simply potting a Christmas pine in a client's living room, Nikki's boundless energy amazes me: as long as you agree with her, of course!

Up at 6 A.M. to get the best at New Covent Garden, the long day often tumbles into a long night for a girl not immune to donning a party frock, as long as it's Marni, Betty Jackson, Céline or Chanel. When staying at Nikki's beautiful home, I often feign illness to catch up on a few hours' sleep and luxuriate in the comfort she surrounds herself with.

Clad in Levi's Red and a Marc Jacobs military jacket behind the wheel of one of her turquoise Wild at Heart vans, the reality of flower arranging is not quite as glamorous as the finished result. From carting crates of lilies to dethorning 1,000 roses, Nikki's approach is totally hands-on. Not only is she active all day

Nikki Tibbles holds a bouquet of lilac-colored sweetpeas in her flower shop, Wild at Heart, in Notting Hill.

and most of the night, she boxes three times a week and simply can't let a Sunday go by without a two-hour gym session or the cooking of a three-course lunch for ten. It's all in a day's work for Tibs. Nikki Tibbles is an inexhaustible shopper. She loves to come home with something. A pack of Cumberland sausages from Tom's Deli will do, but nothing beats a new outfit. Her fashion consumption is approached with a passion rivaling her work ethic.

Her look is casual and comfortable—a collision of stripe and print frequently punctuated with a Birkie clog motif, and lots of cashmere by Fake London, especially the sweaters with an English bull terrier's head on them. The house might be minimal, but the wardrobe space is not.

Nikki is not a broad to be messed with, unless of course you are one of the two girls in Nikki's life—the Battersea babes, Maisie and Rose—then you can do anything. My idea of a heavenly existence would involve reincarnation as one of the aforementioned dogs, or any animal in Nikki's care. While taking the girls for their daily Hampstead Heath jaunt, Nikki transfers the worms on the treacherous path back to a safe earthy place. Which leads me onto her next problem—she is generous to a fault.

What do you regard as the lowest depth of misery?
Emptiness, loneliness.

Where would you like to live?
Where I am, I am very happy, but I would love and strive to live in the middle of nowhere with my dogs and husband (somewhere very hot and beautiful).

What is your idea of earthly happiness?
Walking my dogs, peace, driving my 1970 280SL Mercedes, known as a Mercedes Pagoda.

To what faults do you feel most indulgent?
Spending too much money on clothes.

Who is your favorite hero in real life?
Madonna.

Who are your favorite painters?
Picasso and William Scott.

Who is your favorite musician?
Madonna.

Who is your favorite writer?
Wilkie Collins.

What are the qualities you most admire in a man?
Humor, strength and tenderness.

What are the qualities you most admire in a woman?
Modesty, humor, strength, intelligence, capability, warmth, gentleness.

What are your favorite virtues?
Generosity, honesty.

Who would you have liked to be?
An architect or a vet.

What is your most marked characteristic?
Impatience.

What do you most value in your friends?
Their love and support.

What is your principal defect?
Impatience.

What to your mind would be the greatest of misfortunes?
Being blind or being in prison.

What is your favorite color?
Pink.

What is your favorite bird?
Eagle. If the question is fish, then I would choose bone fish.

Above: Fresh cut roses on the dining room "Tulip" table by Erno, with butterfly chairs by Arnie Jacobsen. The aluminum lamp is by Arco and the painting is a copy of a William Scott.
Far left: A sketch of Nikki Tibbles by London's fashion designer Betty Jackson.
Left: Detail of a collection of vases on a drawing room shelf.

SUE WEBSTER AND TIM NOBLE

BY STUART SHAVE

Since they met at a bus stop in Nottingham in 1986, the lives and loves of Tim Noble and Sue Webster have stopped at nothing short of meteoric. More like the art world's Sid and Nancy than Posh and Beck's, the pair have carved a career out of selling piles of rubbish for cash and America back to the Americans.

A show of art by Tim Noble and Sue Webster at any one time might incorporate any one of the following: monstrous strobes of flashing, pulsating neon, shimmering Las Vegas lightbulbs, the contents of their rubbish bin, a house full of taxidermied animals, vibrators and dildos (which they purchase by the bag load from the seedier side of Soho), plastic flowers, broken crockery, back issues of *Vanity Fair*, real U.S. dollars, plastic tiaras...

This is the "stuff" of their art. The world that surrounds them thus becomes the world that they want it to be, "their" world. In 1998, they inaugurated the first show at our gallery Modern Art Inc. Ltd. with a sculpture comprised of the last six months of their own personal trash. When hit by a light source, this seemingly random pile of detritus offered up the perfect silhouette of the artists onto the gallery wall. The world's biggest art collectors flocked to see this vista, but refused to buy the art because they thought that it would contaminate their homes. These days, they can't get enough of trash, but now they are told they have to wait in line, Oliver Twist style, like everyone else. There simply isn't enough of the cake to go around.

Like the greatest works of pop art, here is all the supermarket packaging of our times sculpted into a random mass that provides the shadow without the figure. The shadow has since become a recurring theme in their works, which always have to be exhibited in a dark room (for this reason Noble and Webster prefer to show in the winter months). Ghosts of their former

selves—the intangible shadows of Tim Noble and Sue Webster—live on in their work, there but not there. A shadow is something, after all, that you can look at but not touch.

Like *West Side Story* or *Romeo and Juliet*, they come from different sides of the tracks. He is the son of an artist from the West Country, she the daughter of an electrician from Leicester (by the way, Webster had learned to wire up entire circuit boards by the time she was 14), yet these two even manage to look so alike that people often think that they are brother and sister rather than husband and wife (except they're not but might as well be). They cut their own hair and live on a diet that ranges between supermarket "own label" baked beans and spaghetti hoops on toast to Veuve Clicquot Champagne, which they guzzle by the bottle-load like deprived gannets. They frequent the local bars of their stomping ground of Shoreditch and are partial to the Francis Bacon–style alcoholic oblivion provided by other bastions of artist drinking holes such as The Colony Rooms and The Groucho Club. Prone to public displays of loving affection as well as violent outbursts, arguments and fistfights, nothing is done by the short measure. More like a triple gin and tonic.

Like some of the best bands that populate their record collection (among them Patti Smith, PJ Harvey and Courtney Love, who is herself a fan of theirs in turn), they also travel in entourage. Recently, Beverly Hills was taken over by a cast of characters including Shoreditch royalty like "Irish Anne" (who, in her gold sequined dress, pole-danced on the table at the most formal of dinners thrown by their Los Angeles gallery). They have a love/hate relationship with the press and once, for the purpose of a TV documentary, agreed to live for a week with an elderly couple of traditional artists to see how they would get on. They didn't. After being fed dinners of fish and chips from the Chinese Chip Shop in Hoxton Street and forced to sleep on a camp bed next to a pile of rubbish, the elderly couple fled back to Surrey for their lives. Tim Noble's mother couldn't go into her local post office for a month, so ashamed was she of her son's behavior on national television. Saying this, all the best bands are usually the bad ones.

It takes a stroke of genius to turn a pile of rubbish into an iconoclastic testament to love, or the tacky lights of Vegas into an eternal promise, but Noble and Webster have managed it. They've done it once and they'll do it again. Over and Out.

Previous page: Sue Webster
and Tim Noble outside their
studio/home in front of their
red Mustang, 1968. "I bought
it from a guy down in Rivington
Street. I call him Mustang
Johnny," says Tim.
Top: Sue and Tim at home
in their studio holding portraits
painted by each other.
Bottom, left to right: Two views
of *Idea wall*, detail of graffiti on
Tim and Sue's studio walls.

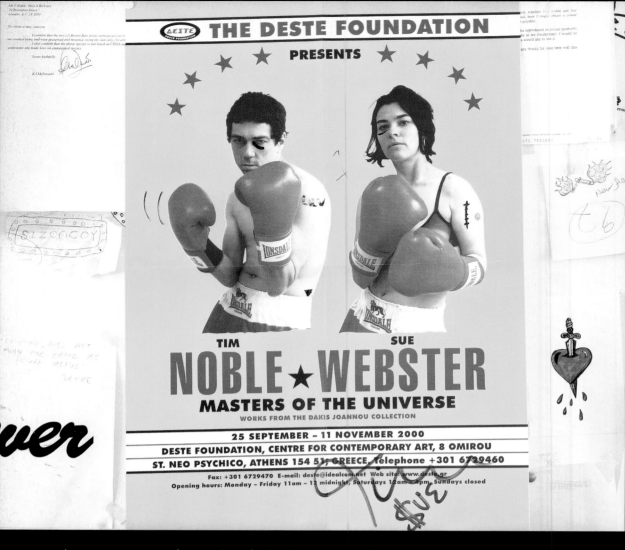

Above: Boxing poster of Tim and Sue for the show "Masters of the Universe," Athens, 2000.
Below: *Vagueus*, mirror-polish stainless steel, white lights and ruby red neon, 1998, illuminates the studio wall at home. Opposite: *$* featured in the November 2001 show of Tim and Sue's work at the Gagosian Gallery in Los Angeles sits in the empty loft space soon to be redesigned as Sue and Tim's studio/home. *The whole year inn*, a neon sign above the window, made by Tim and Sue, 1998, "comes out every time we have a party; we hang it over the bar," says Sue.

Above: *Instant Gratification* (detail), shadow work by Tim and Sue made of U.S. dollars, for a Gagosian gallery show in Los Angeles, November 2001.

Far left: Detail of architect David Adjaye's proposal model for Tim and Sue's studio/home on Chance Street in Shoreditch.

Left: Tim and Sue eagerly await Adjaye's reconstruction of their empty warehouse.

What do you regard as the lowest depth of misery?
Sue: A black hole that just gets deeper and deeper.
Tim: The deepest darkest depths of my imagination.

Where would you like to live?
Sue: In total contentment.
Tim: In Tarzan's tree house.

What is your idea of earthly happiness?
Sue: Being at one with yourself.
Tim: People stopping killing each other would be a good start.

To what faults do you feel most indulgent?
Sue: Discontentment.
Tim: Escapism, excessive sensual indulgence.

Who are your favorite heroes of fiction?
Sue: Thelma and Louise, Nicolas Cage and Laura Dern in *Wild at Heart*.
Tim: The cow and the chicken.

Who are your favorite heroes in real life?
Sue: Bonnie and Clyde, Sid and Nancy.
Tim: Those who break the mold, cross the line, push the silt down the stream.

Who are your favorite characters in history?
Sue: The New Barbarians.
Tim: Same as above.

Who are your favorite musicians?
Sue: Beethoven for his Piano Concerto No. 5 and Symphony No. 7; PJ Harvey, Patti Smith.
Tim: Too many to choose.

Who are your favorite writers?
Sue: Shakespeare for his passages about life as a theatre and for inventing many words in the English language such as "bubble." Bret Easton Ellis for *American Psycho*.

What is the quality you most admire in a man?
Sue: Inner beauty with absolutely no ego.

Tim: I've got jet lag, can't think of one yet...

What is the quality you most admire in a woman?
Sue: PJ Harvey, sexy but talented.
Tim: Vivid imagination, strong personality, sense of humor.

What is your favorite virtue?
Sue: Never to have taken up smoking.
Tim: The jet lag's really kicking in now...

What is your favorite occupation?
Sue: The one that I have.
Tim: er, art...

Who would you have liked to be?
Sue: Someone right in the center of the British punk rock explosion of the mid-seventies—Sid Vicious or Siouxsie Sioux.
Tim: Madonna.

What do you most value in your friends?
Sue: Equality, honesty and respect.
Tim: Honesty, love and respect.

What is your principle defect?
Sue: Absolutely no patience whatsoever.
Tim: Too sensitive.

What to your mind would be the greatest of misfortunes?
Sue: Never to have fully pursued any God-given talent.
Tim: For the world to become void of its extraordinary diversity, of beautiful creatures and be replaced by mediocre bland ones instead.

What is your favorite color?
Sue: Black and white.
Tim: Sky blue.

What is your favorite bird?
Sue: I absolutely adore Mr. and Mrs. Blackbird.
Tim: A free one.

CHRIS CUNNINGHAM

BY LORCAN O'NEILL

There is definitely something messianic about the young film- and video-maker Chris Cunningham. He'd be embarrassed to hear anyone say that—he's genuinely shy and modest—but there has always been an air of mystery and intensity about him. From the early rumors of a prodigy working with Stanley Kubrick, through the years of multi-award-winning videos for Aphex Twin, Madonna and Bjork, to his recent breakthrough into the art world, Cunningham has earned almost reverential respect and admiration from his peers and collaborators. He inspires enthusiastic devotion in a truly global audience that identifies deeply with the beauty and loneliness of his images. He rarely appears in public, and famously skipped the opening party for his first major gallery exhibition in London as well as the glamorously attended festivities for this year's Venice Biennale in which he was included. When he does show up, one is aware of a palpable vulnerability coupled with a cool alertness that underlines his undoubted charisma. Add to this his pale skin, pensive gaze, slender frame and long hair, and you end up with an aura that is certainly poetic, if not downright prophetic.

During his short career, he has won the confidence of some very remarkable men and women. Not many teenagers could have convinced the great Stanley Kubrick to offer them employment. In recent years, Chris has worked from the offices of Ridley Scott, the maker of *Blade Runner*, regarded by many as one of the most influential films of all time. I remember meeting Chris in 1998 when Madonna said she had chosen a young English director to make the video of "Frozen," the first eagerly awaited release from her soon-to-be best-selling album produced with William Orbit. It seemed entirely characteristic of her insight to choose someone then known only by few but already destined for cult status. In an equally perceptive judgment, she also said he was a good artist. And indeed, over the following few years, he navigated with

spectacular success the notoriously difficult waters of the art world. In London, he was taken on by Anthony d'Offay, the city's premier gallery, and was included in last year's Apocalypse exhibition at the Royal Academy.

Fellow filmmaker John Maybury says, "Chris Cunningham's achievement rests on the brilliance with which he has successfully brought to popular culture all the anxiety, rawness and visceral emotion of avant-garde cinema." Experimental film used to be an underground activity, scraped together with tiny budgets and viewed in dingy film clubs and university basements. But Chris is of a generation that has introduced the poor relation to mainstream culture, and he has done it without a hint of vulgarity or condescension. Says Maybury, "Every period has some individuals who turn out work that is truly something else—and everybody notices." Chris has used all the power and clout of commercial filmmaking to bring the highest production values, the most sophisticated editing and the most technically adept special effects to subversive ideas and managed to make them popular. The popular success of his Aphex Twin videos is in spite of the freaky, edgy imagery; the Bjork video works because the beauty and sincerity of the singer/robot is shocking but undeniable; *flex* is violent and erotically unnerving, but rings of simple human truth.

Chris himself epitomizes these qualities. In spite of his success, he's an anomaly in the world in which he moves. Meeting him at work begins like a visit to any successful advertising or film company—all clean, calm-colored reception rooms and bright corridors where attractive young people move quietly around. Then you enter Chris's room, and suddenly you are in what feels like the back-to-the-future laboratory of a brilliant and eccentric scientist. There are piles of papers, doodles, tapes, discs and computer equipment. The room smells as though it has been slept in overnight (which indeed he often does when working on projects), and all around are props and bits of technical hardware from his various films, among them the robot from *All Is Love* and the perfectly sculpted head of a baby for *A.I.*—his contribution to the never-finished film project with Stanley Kubrick. Among all this material, much of which literally comes alive on screen, there is a certain air of isolation. This might be the price he pays for the singularity of his vision, and it's easy to imagine Chris at his computer as a modern Pygmalion, alone in his studio sculpting the perfect female form, or as the brilliant Doctor Frankenstein, determined against all opposition to expand the boundaries of science with his life-giving experiments.

Despite this, there is also a very regular guy inside Chris. He is protective of his privacy in a masculine way, goes home to his family for Christmas, worries for his dad's sake about getting the background details right in interviews and, after working in Italy last year says he can't get the women out of his mind. Right now, as he's finishing a new video for Aphex Twin and preparing to work on new art films, it's this level-headedness that keeps it all in balance and ensures we'll be seeing a lot more of him in the years to come.

Young film and videomaker Chris Cunningham stands alone in the Haunch of Venison Yard, a building used to film one of his videos.

DANIEL DE LA FALAISE

BY MARIANNE FAITHFULL

I've known Dan since he was two years old and playing in a sand-pit in Wales with his sister Lucie. I am a great friend of his parents. Obviously, none of us had any idea that Dan would turn into such a swan. He is a very romantic person, a bit idealistic and needs to come down to earth somewhat, although I myself like idealistic dreamers. It's given me an enormous thrill to see Dan grow up, get real and work hard. From the sandpit, to the stage, to the kitchen, I knew he could do it. He's a fabulous chef and also a great actor. I know we will see him on the stage again.

Dan is very drawn to beauty—beautiful places, beautiful food and beautiful women. He can be a complete cunt and, at the same time, he is incredibly kind. He is a good child. He is a good man. I think it's always been a torment to Dan to be seen as a beautiful social butterfly. In some ways, he really is almost too good-looking to be taken seriously. That is a problem I understand from personal experience. I guess it is difficult for those kinds of kids who you'd expect to have money, yet they actually don't. Dan is certainly not suffering from entitlement. Dan knows that to get through life, you have to work. I call that being a man.

BY ANITA VON PALLENBERG

He's an in-law now; he's part of the family. His sister Lucie married my son, Marlon Richards. We have wonderful times together, all roaming through the countryside. He and Lucie are extremely close. I met them both at an Anna Sui opening in New York years before Lucie married my son. They were huddled together, so gorgeous looking. I always wanted a brother like Dan. He is very witty, modern, yet very romantic like all the de la Falaises. He's always immaculate in that dandy kind of way, always wearing velvet

Daniel de la Falaise, a chef at his uncle Mark Birley's club George, sits in front of an unfinished painting Birley bought at auction. Most of the works in the club are by David Hockney.

somewhere. He's a fantastic cook, and I am so looking forward to him preparing our Christmas dinner. He has found his passion for food as a chef, and I am thrilled for him.

BY MARK BIRLEY

I am very devoted to Daniel. He's my grand nephew and he's working as a second chef at George. I think he has been cooking since he was six years old. He's been brought up in an atmosphere of cooking and food and my sister Maxime de la Falaise, Daniel's grandmother, has had an enormous influence on him as she cooks such extraordinary things. Right now, Daniel's been working with a lot of Italians and has picked up the language and the cuisine. He's really such an asset and a wonderful ally!

Alec
McCowen

&
Clem

a new play by
...hen Churchett

with

...arah Woodward
Daniel de la Falaise

Directed by
Richard Wilson

Designed by
Rob Howell

Jo...

Lighting by
Mick Hughes

Aldwych Th...
Aldwych, London, WC2B 4D...
0171-416 6007
...M Nederlander Under the Management...

GEORGE

"THE WEST END
AT ITS BEST!"
Kaleidoscope, BBC Radio 4
"A HIGH THEATRICAL DELIGHT
A DELICIOUS COMIC-SATIRICAL FRAMEWORK AND
TOWERING PERFORMANCES FROM
MICHAEL
GAMBON & ALEC
McCOWEN"
Nicholas de Jongh, Evening Standard

Tom & Clem
A new play by
Stephen Churchett
with
Sarah Woodward   Daniel de la Falai...
Designed by Rob Howell
Lighting by Mick Hughes   Sound by John A Le...
Directed by
Richard Wilson

ALDWYCH THEATRE
ALDWYCH LONDON WC2

Daniel de la Falaise (Alexei), Michael Gambon (Tom Driberg) and Alec McCowen (Clement Attlee) in Stephen Churchett's excellent debut as a playwright, Tom and Cle...

Above: Daniel's keepsakes: a poster and playbill from *Tom & Clem*, in which Daniel played a Russian KGB officer; a photograph of Daniel and Madonna's breast taken by Steven Meisel for Madonna's *SEX* book; a Cecil Beaton photograph of Daniel's grandmother Maxime de la Falaise; a political cartoon review in *The Times* of *Tom & Clem*. Far left: Daniel and his uncle, Mark Birley, in front of Mark's new club, George, on South Audley Street. Left: Daniel's famous white shoes. "I've been wearing them since I'm 15," says Daniel.

We have lunch and dinner together quite often and he tells me many stories of his love life. It has been quite varied I must say. I have never seen his photo in Madonna's *SEX* book; he is rather coy about the whole thing. He is quite photogenic and looks so smart in his whites when he's all dressed for work. But he has little time to play these days. He's got a car and little flat I gave him, but has no time to socialize. I know he's on his way to being a fabulous chef, as his heart is really in it.

What do you regard as the lowest depth of misery?
The tube at rush hour, and microwave meals.

What is your idea of earthly happiness?
Oysters on an empty stomach.

To what faults do you feel most indulgent?
Nicotine.

Who is your favorite hero of fiction?
Marina Gorky.

Who are your favorite heroes in real life?
Shepherds and shepherdesses.

Who are your favorite characters in history?
Edgar Cayce, Adelle Davis, T.C. Lethbridge.

Who is your favorite painter?
Victoria FitzWilliam Lay.

Who is your favorite musician?
Johnny Johnson, who was Chuck Berry's piano player.

Who is your favorite writer?
Colin Wilson.

What is your favorite occupation?
Feeding people, especially children.

Who would you have liked to be?
A pilot.

What is your most marked characteristic?
White shoes. I've been wearing them since I've been 15!

What do you most value in your friends?
Complicity.

What is your principal defect?
Temper.

What to your mind would be the greatest of misfortunes?
Malnutrition.

What is your favorite color?
Green.

What are your favorite birds?
The kingfisher and the heron.

Daniel buying produce for George, at the Borough Market near London Bridge.

DARCEY BUSSELL

BY DONALD MCLEARY

AND MONICA MASON

Donald McLeary and I have watched Darcey since she was a student at the Royal Ballet School.

Since she joined the company, we have both worked with her a great deal, and in describing her, we have decided on a rave review.

She is a professional to her toe-tips and is enormous fun to be with in her studio. She has always been eager to learn and takes her work very seriously. She invites criticism, is highly motivated, but very generous and gregarious. Her natural charm endears her to everyone who meets her, and that makes her a great ambassador for the company. She has a wonderful sense of humor and lives life to the full, both in and out of the theatre. She has a very practical side to her nature, which enables her to keep calm under pressure. She has a great sense of style—we both think she's a natural star!

Darcey Bussell, prima ballerina of London's Royal Ballet, in a white tulle "practice tutu" rises on point backstage with crew at the Royal Opera House.

Above: Darcey in her dressing room, her home away from home. Letters and photographs from fans adorn the mirror and walls. Opposite: Piles of shellacked pink toe shoes. Each principal dancer has three to four pairs ready per performance.

Where would you like to live?
I would like to live by a warm sea.

What is your idea of earthly happiness?
Lying on a deserted beach.

To what faults do you feel most indulgent?
Eating chocolate and buying things for my daughter Phoebe.

Who is your favorite hero of fiction?
Penelope Pitstop.

Who is your favorite hero in real life?
Audrey Hepburn.

07 D Bussell

*Who are your favorite
characters in history?*
Sir Walter Raleigh and Michelangelo.

Who are your favorite painters?
Too many favorites, but in particular Anna Pinkster.

Who is your favorite musician?
I have many, but some of them would be,
and I know this is cheating but,
Rachmaninoff, Vivaldi, Mozart, Fauré,
Freddie Mercury and Lenny Kravitz.

What is the quality you most admire in a man?
Calmness and modesty.

What is the quality you most admire in a woman?
Independence.

What is your favorite virtue?
Diligence.

What is your most marked characteristic?
Stubbornness.

What do you most value in your friends?
Loyalty and caring.

What is your principal defect?
I am a fidget.

What to your mind would be the greatest of misfortunes?
Never to be in love.

What is your favorite color?
Lilac, at the moment.

What are your favorite birds?
Hummingbird and flamingo.

Darcey poised before the stage of the newly refurbished Royal Opera House.

PHILIP TREACY

INTERVIEW BY ISABELLA BLOW

Actually, when you talk about flat…

Well, apartment…

Well, apartment, I've just been to the exhibition of an artist, something called "Super Flat," by Tukishike Rurenkana.

Have you seen the bed in the Victoria and Albert Museum?

Which one?

The red velvet bed.

Oh it's amazing, it's incredible, the one from Hampton Court. It's my favorite bed. What is it you like about it?

It's just bonkers; it's like a skyscraper.

You mean it is the proportions that drive you crazy.

It is such a bizarre proportion, I'm sure it would be like being in a building. Can you imagine lying in bed where the roof is so tall?

Was it a very famous red bed?

Yes. But what is so interesting is you've just said the word I could never put my finger on. Building. It's just like a building.

Well, Detmar's grandfather, the architect—so like you, he understood proportion—designed the bed for this house, it was the same thing. It was hitting the roof, like a building. He made buildings, and you make hats. Obviously, it's that you've picked something that really is full of aesthetics, and it really is one of the most beautiful things I've ever seen certainly in terms of reaching to the sky. I say to the sky and you say like a building, which is much more sensible. So you went to that, and red, you like red because, what does red mean to you?

Red is exciting.

And does it have anything to do with religion?

Not that kind of red, but all the colors I like are…

Spiritual.

Not really spiritual, they're very religious colors, Catholic colors—scarlet, purples and gold.

Portrait of world famous hat designer Philip Treacy at home in his pink dining room with his Jack Russell, Mr. Pig.

Above: The coffee table in the royal blue sitting room holds two glass-encased treasures, a paper model of Louis XIV, and a French 18th-century wedding headdress, along with photos of Mr. Pig and model Kirsten McMenany in one of Philip's designs.
Opposite: Philip sits with Mr. Pig in the acid green stairwell. Model Suzy Bick chose the palette throughout the interior. Nestled on stairwell shelf are two of Philip's hat designs, a large black straw hat, and a forest top hat made of earth and twigs.

Is that because when you first used your imagination, as I did, it was in church? I don't know if you find it an inspiring place...

It is a very inspiring place, but for me it's more in your subconscious, so I like very specific colors and never thought why I liked the colors. Then I started seeing them in churches, they were just colors I grew up with. There's something untouchable about those colors. It's the mad intensity of the colors.

How old were you when you made your first hat?

I was 18.

You hadn't done any drawings previously but you'd watch people wearing hats.

I never thought about them inasmuch as I didn't think it would be interesting to make hats. It first happened when I started making clothes.

And you always felt they needed something on top, or what?

I liked the idea of making a hat with it, and just started it as a hobby.

And then when you did, you realized it was an obsession, or rather when did you decide to put strength into the head rather than the rest of the body?

I found I could make a hat, not because it was easy but more because it wasn't that difficult.

What was your first hat?

It was a matador's hat made from an old straw hat that I got in a junk shop in Dublin.

Wow, what did you love about it?

I discovered that materials could turn into other things through this material. Your hands shape it.

I love the idea of hand-shaping. Everything you do, of course, is shaped by your hand, which makes it so exquisite.

Well, everything I'm about is handwork, so it is all about the love one puts into making something. It is the most exciting thing in the world, making something from nothing. It is food for the soul.

Boys weren't encouraged to use the sewing machine, but your teacher felt your talent, and it was exciting to develop the passion, drowned by the noise of your mother feeding the chickens.

Yes, not that she'd have been livid.

You have this love of feathers and textures of birds and things like that, so that must have happened when you were little, watching them running around.

We grew up with pheasants, chickens, geese and things like that, but I didn't really think of them, of really making things in terms of the feathers, they were just around. But later, I started to use feathers and just thought they were the most incredible material on earth, because they are a living material.

Do you get what they call a feedback?

Yes, absolutely, it's just the most incredible material I've ever encountered.

Oh, I know. We're sitting here in your flat and I've been asked to ask to reveal a few things about your internal life, your working creative life. Garbo: what is your creative fascination for her? You've got these amazing photographs of her. What is it about her?

I don't really have a fascination about Garbo, but I just love those black-and-white, quintessential Hollywood glamour shots I found in a junk shop in Malibu. They're a prototype of glamour photography that is in all our daily lives today. Some of them are like drag; some of them are pastiche, not all of them.

What is your favorite piece she wore?

She wore a great hat.

Was it Queen Christina?

It was a tube hat.

The thing is, most people think the usual things, oh, the Mad Hatter, a hat to look formal, a hat to do this, a hat to do that, but actually what you've done is you've made the hat a part of the person or the person part of the hat. That's what's given them so much pleasure—they feel they've been able to enhance their own beauty through you, and you've managed to make it modern through the lightness of the material. No one ever feels they're carrying a boulder on their head. The old thing was "I've got to wear a hat and it's so heavy" and you've made it so modern and fascinating for people. I've always said you are like Dalí, and if they buy a piece they've got a unique thing for them, so you've managed to push through all these incredible boundaries of hat wearing. And you're getting into men, too.

Men wear hats, too. Many women wear hats for men.

Yes. Dietrich wore the man's hat, Saint Laurent and all that.

A hat is empowering, as was that look. It's very elegant.

Yes, I always find it no problem to get a table at a restaurant, or a taxi in the rain in a hat, because people immediately assume you're the queen, they assume you have some important status. You're treated differently. And people who wear hats feel good about themselves.

I've met so many people through hats.

I have too. You either get a dog or a hat. They protect you. They're great protective pieces, the hats. I love the

Above, left: Philip Treacy's boutique on Elizabeth Street. Above, right: Hand-carved wooden hat blocks made in Paris and used for each of Philip's designs.

empowerment thing; they're like magic. You put it on your head and it immediately makes you feel better.

That's exactly what I love about hats. Hats are magic. They bring out emotions in people.

A reaction.

Exactly, you sure get a reaction. People can either love it or loathe it, but no other accessory has the same spice of life as a hat does. When you're wearing a hat, people look at your face, not your toes. It's a very potent thing to wear.

When you mention that word "potent," I think of mystery, beauty and sex, because that's how lure your victim.

And that's what hats are all about.

It's a good as any pet, but more of an ice breaker. Look how many people you've made feel good. It's been a fantastic tonic, after September 11th; we can feel your human touch. Fashion is becoming about human touch; people want individual pieces made to make them feel better. This is a perfect time to make craft as you do with the future.

Craft has a fantastic future, because we're surrounded by technology. We live with it every day. But in fact, the most precious things in a futuristic context are things someone's put some emotion into, not a machine that's stamped it out. In a way, we thought clothes in the future would be stamped out. But in fact what's happening is that people want something especially for them.

It's about the human touch. When you've been in hospital and had someone holding your hand, you understand that human contact can carry you through any operation because you have the support and love. That's exactly the same principle in hats, when you feel someone has really thought about this and you can feel the emotions in the design.

You can't explain why you want it or you need it.

It's desire, one of the strongest human emotions. It's an emotion that's made people have babies, no one can explain why or how, but it happens. It's just one of those things. You can have desire for many people and many things, and once you get hit by the hat, it's a new desire that is attainable. You just go into to the shop and buy it.

ROBERT VIOLETTE

BY PAUL SMITH

Over the years, I have been approached many times by publishers, usually interested in some unimaginative retrospective of my collections. When Robert first contacted me to discuss a book, my attitude was much the same: I couldn't really see the point. But then, after we talked, and talked again, it was apparent that Robert had a different view. In the same way that I like to approach designing clothes from a sideways perspective, putting the wrong thing with the wrong thing to create something new and surprising, Robert absolutely did not want to make a "fashion book." Seeing the marvelous art books that Robert had already created, I became convinced that we had a chance to make something unexpected. Robert's background is unconventional for a publisher. For eight years, he edited and produced books at the Anthony d'Offay Gallery, including the first book by Jeff Koons and important artists' writings books by Gerhard Richter and Bill Viola. With Violette Editions, set up in 1997, he has published thoughtful books, including writings by Louise Bourgeois and Gilbert & George, *Double Game* by Sophie Calle, an edition by Francesco Vezzoli, and he has championed the iconoclastic British artist Leigh Bowery. His forthcoming titles include collaborations with architect Frank O. Gehry, artist Doug Aitken and writer Marina Warner.

When Robert and I started working together, we had little idea where we were headed, apart from a shared aim to make a book that possessed a little bit of Paul Smith attitude, now entitled *You Can Find Inspiration in Everything*. After more than two years, Robert ended up as far away from a typical fashion book as one can get—a book that includes a polystyrene case designed by Jonathan Ive, designer of the iMac; eleven different papers; thirty-five different covers bound in Paul Smith printed fabrics; an introduction by self-described "psychogeographer" William Gibson; a factual "story" by sportswriter Richard Williams; a fiction by novelist James Flint; interviews with a neuroscientist and an art curator; as well as texts by me. Not a fashion writer in sight! This book even includes two posters, a magnifier and a comic book. It's the result of Robert's intense personal involvement, an approach that I know is typical of all the projects he undertakes.

Another reason I think Robert was interested in working with me was that he could see parallels in how we both approach business—our independence and not giving into the mainstream. Mine is a personal company, run with passion, a sense of humor and, I hope, occasional ingenuity, but also with a keen eye to developing the business. I see signs of that in what Robert is doing with his company. He never hurries his ideas into print and always remains willing to alter things, to improve things, even at the last minute. There's some sort of perfectionism at work here. I've never met a publisher with the same vision, dedication and sheer guts. And that, I imagine, has to be rare.

BEN ELLIOT

BY LUCIA VAN DER POST

If there's one thing guaranteed to make Ben Elliot cross, it's the "top toff" tag. But if your aunt is Camilla Parker Bowles, you've been educated at Eton and your intimate circle includes Goldsmiths, Rothschilds and Parker Bowleses, it's one that's going to be hard to shift. It probably explains the "mockney" accent, the slightly louche suits, the Cuban shirts ("I buy them from a chap with a lock-up in Woking") and the addiction to Tottenham Hotspurs.

But he's right to be cross—behind the handy catch-all label lurks a much more complex figure. Apart from anything else, he's already done more than any 26-year-old has a right to. Not for him the smart merchant bank, the bar or a fashionable job in the media. He's looked after orphans in Romania, worked on a building site and helped run Jimmy Goldsmith's Referendum Party. Straight from Bristol University, he set about his career as a budding tycoon. He plunged into partnership with nightclub entrepreneur Piers Adam ("When I met him," says Piers, "I just fell in love with him"), helping to develop a new breed of cool nightclubs and bars (one is rumored to be the place where Prince William knocked back his first public drink). Then it was on to something just as cool—fluid juice bars. He divined that wheatgrass, cranberry juice, ginger and ginseng were what the health-conscious skinny Voguettes would want to be drinking, so he snapped up a plum site right next door to Vogue House.

That would be more than enough to keep most 25-year-olds busy, but not Ben. Before he turned 26, he was on to the venture that is currently occupying most of his waking moments. "Quintessentially" is a members' club dedicated to looking after the day-to-day problems, the travels, the fun and the entertainment of those who are too busy or preoccupied to do it for

Ben Elliot on the Kensington Gardens bandstand, built in 1931 by J.H. Markham, often used in the summer by the Royal College of Music.

themselves and are happy to pay £400 a year to have somebody do it for them. To get it off the ground took countless sleepless nights, loads of hard work, much networking and enough persuasiveness to charm money out of the moneymen and working partnerships out of a wide range of clubs, spas, hotels and suppliers. In a mere eight months, he got it up and running. These days, it has a membership list that most clubs would kill for.

Not only has Ben done more in his 26 years than most men have done in 40, he seems to know most of London, too, which, for somebody who claims to be a Dorset boy and who only arrived in London full-time after he'd left university, is something of a feat. From the doormen at Aspinall's (where most weeks he plays poker with the people he's closest to—his cousin Tom Parker Bowles, Zac Goldsmith, Michael Gove of *The Times* and a few other chosen intimates) to Jesus at The Caprice, Gordon Campbell Grey of One Aldwych, every PR girl and the grandest in the land, Ben seems to know them all. He talks as easily to the man behind the bar as to merchant bankers. His friends range from designers and socialites to football fans and journalists, from pop stars and television personalities to aristocrats and ambassadors. He's just as appealing to men as to women, and his friendships cross the age gaps. They may all be greeted with the same easy charm, but if one of them is in trouble, he's the first to lift the phone.

On weekends, he's often found shooting with landed gentry in the winter, playing cricket at Sudeley Castle in the summer, off for a long weekend in Ibiza or the south of France or staying with his family—to whom he remains very close—down in Dorset.

He has huge enthusiasms and does nothing by halves. He's obsessed with boxing. "Play it like a butterfly, sting like a bee" could be said to be his motto. He reads every book and watches every movie remotely connected with the ring.

He knows he's been dealt a privileged hand. "I've been lucky," he says. "All my life, interesting people have been coming to our house, and I've been inspired by many of them. I've always greatly admired Mark Birley, for instance, with his fastidious taste and his attention to detail. That's the sort of fastidiousness that I want to bring to Quintessentially. Both my parents have their own businesses (his mother, Annabel Elliot, is renowned for her "eye" and has a share in one of England's most charming antique shops, Talisman in Gillingham, Dorset, while his father runs a number of different businesses, including a cabinetmaking one), so I think the entrepreneurial gene is in the blood."

While his appeal to some of the most attractive girls in town remains undiminished, just watch them come floating up in restaurants, at parties, or any of the myriad places where Ben is to be found of a night—for the moment, his mind is firmly on building his business. He's the first to admit that he's restless, easily bored—"I need to feel passionate about something if I'm going to be effective. I can only do the boring things if I really care about what I'm doing."

As a child, Ben was obsessed with magic. "Mervin the Marvel," they called him in the family as he, with Tom Parker Bowles as his able assistant, pulled his rabbits out of hats at family do's. Mervin the Marvel may be temporarily on hold, but Ben is still busy weaving magic—only now it's up in London town. A space, as they say, to watch.

TARA SUMMERS

BY MICHAEL LINDSAY HOGG

The first time I saw Tara, she was sitting on a sofa making eyes at me. She had a blanket wrapped around her, not because she wasn't feeling well, but because she was only one and a half years old. Her mother had taken her out of bed so we could meet, and then her mother left the room to make a cup of tea. Tara and I sat looking at each other and trying to communicate. I know that's what we were trying to do, because I could tell from her expression and smile and sense of enthusiasm that in the mind of this pretty baby was a lively social intelligence trying to connect. I spoke to her the way I thought was right, not in goo-goo language, thinking to do that was somehow patronizing, but rather about what was going on in London that day. She blinked and nodded wisely at appropriate times, as though she was taking in what I was saying, and every so often would shine a beatific smile my way as if to encourage me to continue blathering away with my tales of the town. Even then, you knew you were in the presence of a female person. Then her mother returned and carried her back to bed.

As Tara started to grow, she was subject to some of the stresses of a child who has two different front doors to welcome her. I remember her one day with her back pressed up against the inside of one of these doors. We had for some weeks been play-ing a very successful game, from my point of view anyway, in which I had convinced her that I knew Superman, the real one, not Christopher Reeve, who was a friend of her mother. I forget the intricacies of the game, but not the determined five-year-old as she barred the way, folded her arms, planted her little feet firmly in the carpet and wouldn't let me out till I told her the truth. And, as she got older, the truth was always what she wanted. It's interesting she has for years wanted to act, because acting is an endless search for the truth. In the years that followed, Tara became, as can sometimes happen, the unwished-for

175

What do you regard as the lowest depth of misery?
Losing all your friends and cigarettes.

Where would you like to live?
Bali, Costa Rica, Ireland, New York City.

What is your idea of earthly happiness?
Eating buttered popcorn on the beach in Bali.

To what faults do you feel most indulgent?
Cigarettes, fruitcake, taxis.

Who are your favorite heroes of fiction?
Scarlett O'Hara, Boemoth, Oagny Taggart, James Bond.

Who are your favorite heroes in real life?
Martin Summers, Nona Summers, Rudolph Giuliani.

Who are your favorite characters in history?
Elizabeth I, Winston Churchill.

Who are your favorite painters?
Andy Warhol, Balthus, Chris Offili, Lucien Freud, Matisse.

Who are your favorite musicians?
Tchaikovsky, Bob Marley, Notorious BIG.

What is the quality you most admire in a woman?
Lack of pettiness, loyalty.

What is your favorite virtue?
Integrity.

What are your favorite occupations?
Dancing, acting, eating buttered popcorn.

What is your most marked characteristic?
An independent spirit.

What do you most value in your friends?
A sense of humor, comfort, honesty, loyalty.

What is your principal defect?
Messiness, competitiveness.

What to your mind would be the greatest of misfortunes?
To be a virgin all of your life.

What is your favorite color?
Blue.

What is your favorite bird?
Red robin.

witness to examples of adult frailty and misbehavior. And while always retaining the characteristics of a regular nine-, ten- or eleven-year old, she was able to deal with what came her way with a tough intelligence and an unusual degree of sympathy, if sometimes an exasperated one.

Then Heathfield in Berkshire and Brown in Rhode Island, making good grades and good friends. Now acting and having already written and performed a one-woman show, Tara has taken the best of her father's dashing Cavalier nature and her mother's joie de vivre and brains to become a really interesting talented sympathetic charmer, still with the smile that will seduce whatever and whoever is lucky enough to come to stand before her.

Page 174: Tara Summers and her friend Lola Peploe, Bernardo Bertolucci's niece, both aspiring actresses photographed in Nona Summers's drawing room in the heart of Chelsea.

Previous page: Tara Summers's bedroom!

Opposite: A bulletin board outside Tara's room filled with snaps of family friends: Diane von Furstenberg, David Bowie and Nona Summers, David Hockney and Maurice Tuchman, Tara and Kelly Lynch sunbathing by Kelly's pool in Los Angeles, and a Christmas card to Tara from her godfather, Jack Nicholson.

Above: Portrait of Tara Summers, Brown University graduate and student at LAMDA school of acting. Right: Casper the friendly ghost, tattoo done in New York by Squid from the Lunar Chicks, peaks out above Tara's Masai Mara silver, seed,

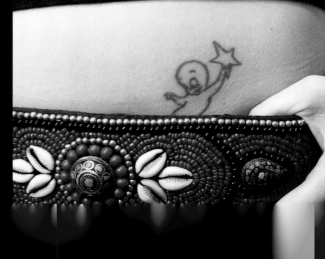

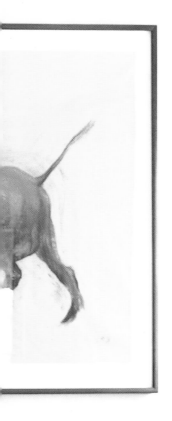

WILLIAM TURNER AND EMILY OPPENHEIMER

BY CATHERINE OSTLER

One winter's night, film producer William Turner sat down at the wrong table in a Notting Hill restaurant and met the artist and girl-about-town Emily Oppenheimer. She giggled at his nonchalance... and the rest is London social history.

Four years later, they're married, with a 3-month-old baby boy, Marlowe, and living in their chic, white townhouse—an oasis of New York style (and a streak of Africa) in the middle of Chelsea. William has left Carlton TV and now works as head of Sky's film and TV making division, Sky Pictures (although he's currently on sabbatical at Harvard Business School), and although Emily still paints, she's also bringing her connections and good humor to her new job as a contributing editor of *Harper's & Queen*.

Much in their new family house reflects Emily's love of art and of horses. In the bedroom, there's an Elizabeth Frink water-color of a galloping horse that Emily's sister, Sophie Oppenheimer, an art buyer, bought at auction, and a Stanley Spencer pencil drawing of a carthorse she bought at Islington Art Fair. Emily admits she is mad about racehorses, as she should be: De Beers, the Oppenheimer family firm, sponsors Diamond Day at Ascot, and her father is a breeder.

But you might spot signs of cinematography, too. There's a huge variety of books and piles of hopeful scripts screaming "read me" in Will's study and two huge black-and-white photographs up the stairs signed by Terry O'Neill: Peter Sellers pulling a face behind a camera and Frank Sinatra strolling down a pier with his bodyguards, looking every inch the leader of the Pack.

Emily wanted their house to have a neutral and uncluttered

Will Turner sits in his drawing room holding son Marlowe, next to his wife, Emily Oppenheimer. Behind them is a Nicola Hicks painting on parcel paper of a wild boar. The carved wooden fish in the foreground is made of driftwood by an artist in South Africa.

Left: A charcoal portrait by Lucien Freud of Bella Freud hangs above two still life works of fruit by Emily, a bronze horse and rider by Elizabeth Frink (commissioned by De Beers) and a photo of Emily's mother, Penny, at Royal Ascot, 1976. The black-and-white photo in the foreground is a party picture of Emily with friends Tamara Beckwith and Tamara Mellon. Above: A Johnny Yeo portrait of Emily, given to Will as an anniversary gif, rests next to a vase of white tulips in the bedroom.

feel, but there's elegance and opulence in the details. Will and Emily commissioned the Venetian mirrors in the sitting room from the London firm Mediterraneo Ltd., who works with a factory on the island of Murano in Venice. They are modern glass, treated to look old, with a blue glass stripe: the inspiration came from the Maharajah of Jaipur's (Bubbles) home, The City Palace, where they visited on their honeymoon. Will found the bamboo coffee table in a tiny shop in St. Tropez; Emily's father has a house nearby they visit every summer, and often on weekends. The lizard side tables are made of acrylic and Macassar ebony and are designed by David Linley. The big sculptured fish (or is he a whale?) is made out of indigenous wood by the African artist Jackson Hlungwane. There is a vase of porcupine needles on the table too—Emily collects one every time they go to the African bush, staying at her cousin's game park in South Africa (their wedding last summer had an African theme, complete with birdsong and lighting like the starry sky over the bush). There are also some of Emily's still lifes, and a huge picture of a wild boar by Nicola Hicks, who's painted Tony Blair. A bronze nanny goat by English sculptress Olivia Musgrave sits in the bookcase. It's from Emily's favorite art gallery in Johannesburg, the Everard Read Gallery.

There is also a striking painting of Bella by Lucien Freud. There is a turban lurking in the bookcase, too, which Bubbles had made for Will. And here is a big, state-of-the-art plasma TV screen, clearly a professional necessity for a producer. In their bedroom, white curtains and the white rabbit-fur rug on the bed (the rug belonged to Emily's grandmother) offset the dark mahogany of the curtain poles and the sleigh bed and the brown crocodile chaise by Fendi. The three-foot-high Art Deco lamps, whose

What do you regard as the lowest depth of misery?
Emily: A broken heart.
Will: Being away from my family for ten weeks.

What is your ideal of earthly happiness?
Emily: Galloping my horse across Watership Down.
Will: Holding my wife and son.

To what faults do you feel most indulgent?
Emily: Buying art.
Will: Good food and wine.

Who are your favorite heroes of fiction?
Emily: Bilbo Baggins, Merlin.
Will: Harrison Ford in *Blade Runner*.

Who are your favorite painters?
Emily: Michelangelo, Caravaggio, Lucien Freud, Matisse, Mark Rothko, de Staël.
Will: Mark Rothko, Marc Chagall, Emily Oppenheimer.

Who is your favorite musician?
Emily: Van Morrison.
Will: Bob Dylan.

Who is your favorite writer?
Emily: Anne Rice, Richard Adams.
Will: Paul Scott, Jay Mcinerney, Joseph Conrad, Thomas Hardy.

What do you most value in your friends?
Emily: Friendship.
Will: Loyalty.

What is your favorite color?
Emily: Indigo blue.
Will: Green.

What is your favorite bird?
Emily: African hawk eagle.
Will: Jonathan Livingston Seagull.

Where would you like to live?
Emily: Half the year in London and the other half in the South African bush and the English countryside.
Will: In the South African bush, New Hampshire, in a tree house.

effect is accentuated by the mirrored bedside tables, come from Valerie Wade. Will's classic leather desk in his study is from one of Emily's favorite shops, Andrew Martin in Walton Street. But the artwork in the study is anything but predictable.

There's a topless painting of Emily in there to distract him (by Johnny Yeo, the talented portrait painter, and a friend, whose painting of Tony Blair has recently been unveiled), and a picture of a bear shoot, a present from Emily that she bought on their honeymoon. There's a Matt Collishaw—girls' faces from porn mags superimposed by pink flowers. Unsurprisingly for a girl who was once a fashion assistant on *Vogue* ("caused mayhem!" she says) and a fashion stylist, Emily's good taste extends to her wardrobe. Anoushka Hempel, who made her wedding dress, is her favorite couturier. As an artist, she loves bright colors, such as pears painted in purple and green and orange. Paradoxically in this house, the only concession to color is in Marlowe's cozy bedroom. His walls are lilac, his sofa is red and his blind, from Designer's Guild, has rabbits on it. He also has a spotty Damien Hirst painting to giggle at. A six-foot-long brown silk snake, a present from Emily's father ("That's his sense of humor," she says) hangs off the bookcase. The Turner-Oppenheimer style might appear glamorously pared down, but it is full of objects that redound with history, and friendship, and the story of their own romance.

FLEUR COWLES

BY ELIZABETH GAGE

As a designer of jewelry, I spend a great deal of my creative time handling and looking closely at a stone and thinking what is the best—the most beautiful—object to which I can convert it. When I was approached and asked to write an appreciation of my very good friend Fleur Cowles, I asked myself whether I could reverse my usual train of thought in order to analyze what made Fleur so special.

Fleur left Boston for New York as a beautiful, very clever young woman with a brilliant memory, total shape and color recall and a talent for writing. Journalism fascinated her, and she wrote a daily column for a New York City newspaper (and also found time to learn to fly and sail boats).

The outbreak of the Second World War needed the adventurous and the brave. Fleur, having passed the American Air Force Navigation Test (almost unheard-of for a woman in the 1940s), became a ferry pilot, mainly delivering important VIPs to Washington in small to medium-sized planes. This was an entrée to the politically famous and powerful. It seemed to be almost a matter of course that Fleur got herself sent to France just as Paris was being recaptured by the Allies, in order to report to the Famine Emergency Committee on the immediate civilian needs relating to food.

As the war ended, the tempo of life changed. Fleur married the attractive and very rich Mike Cowles, who ran a television newspaper and magazine empire. The magazine *Look* was the centerpiece of that empire. Fleur set about improving not only the magazine but the quality of its readership, quadrupling its circulation to nearly seven million.

One of the great highlights of Fleur's creative life was in 1950 when she was let loose to produce *Flair*, the magazine of her dreams. *Flair* was a tremendous artistic success, but it closed after a year because of lack of advertising and the advent of the

184

Korean War. But it left its mark. Even today, a collection of *The Best of Flair* is a best-seller. Copies of the original are collector's trophies. The University of Texas considers Fleur to be the first of great American women magazine editors and the first person to make a magazine into an art form.

Being the editor of an important magazine steered Fleur towards politics. She eventually became a confidante of both Truman and Eisenhower (representing the latter in Brazil, Egypt, Greece, Cyprus and Iran) and was delighted when nominated with General Marshall as Ambassador to the Coronation in London of Queen Elizabeth II.

London seemed to have attracted Fleur, because in 1955 after parting from Mike Cowles, she married a dashing Englishman, Tom Montague Meyer, and has lived in England ever since.

She seemed to have welcome the changed pace from frenetic New York to more peaceful London, where she soon made many good friends and gained a well-deserved reputation as a leading hostess. More importantly, she now had time to paint and write, and her personal creative life flourished. She has written twenty books and has had fifty-eight one-woman exhibitions as a painter.

Purposely, I have left the personal side of Fleur to the last: she is the best friend to many people and has a wonderful ability to bring the best out of almost everybody, even out of a dull dinner party.

Lastly, on a professional note, she is the only one of my close friends who designs not only her own clothes but her own jewelry. As a professional, I have a great admiration for her taste.

A truly remarkable woman—a renaissance woman ahead of her time.

Previous page: Fleur Cowles in her home office. On the bookcase behind her desk is a framed copy of the red cover of *Flair*, Fleur's magazine of twelve issues from 1950.
Opposite: Stacked plates, cups and saucers of Limoges china in a Fleur Cowles' pattern taken from a painting in her front hall, available at Goode in London.
Hanging beside the bookcase is Fleur's first painting, done in a London hospital in 1955, of a clay pot, growing vines and flowers on a wall beside the sea. Fleur was named a senior fellow at the Royal College of Art in London, as documented in the framed certificate hung on the bookcase shelf.
Next pages, far right: Fleur stands before panels of exotic trees in terra-cotta urns painted by Prince Palovicini, commissioned by Fleur, 1954, Rome. Six of the panels act as shutters, five as wall hangings. The numerous framed canvases of Fleur's work await to be sent to the Wildenstein Gallery in New York for an exhibition in November 2001.

This page, top right: The azure blue drawing room where Fleur and her husband Tom Meyer entertain. Collected objets d'art adorn the coffee table in front of a painted glass screen from Austria. To the left of the fireplace are two of the only embroidered works done by Braque in 1954. Below, center and near right: Fleur and Tom spent more than a year re-creating the 1780s ceiling detail, which had been extensively damaged by a World War II bomb. The bookcases and intricate cornices, designed by Fleur, were added later on. A carved and painted wooden Madonna from Marseille, originally a ship's figurehead, hangs high on the wall above the sofa. Bottom, left: One of an unusual pair of table lamps with a tree trunk base in the drawing room, Chinese, found in an antique shop in Peking and made of iron. A collection of small Venetian glass vases, byblos and a Spanish carved wooden figure of Madonna and child fill the surface of the small table top. "There's something from every country in the world in this room," says Fleur with a smile.

What do you regard as the lowest depth of misery?
A night without sleep.

What is your idea of earthly happiness?
Peace of mind.

To what fault do you feel most indulgent?
Smoking.

Who is your favorite hero in real life?
Mother Teresa.

Who is your favorite character in history?
Cleopatra.

Who are your favorite painters?
Dalí or Picasso.

Who is your favorite musician?
Yehudi Menuhin.

Who is your favorite writer?
Rebecca West.

What is the quality you most admire in a man?
Faithfulness.

What is the quality you most admire in a woman?
Sincerity.

What is your favorite occupation?
Painting.

Who would you have liked to be?
Myself.

What is your most marked characteristic?
Selectivity.

What do you most value in your friends?
Affection.

What to your mind would be the greatest of misfortunes?
Loneliness.

What are your favorite colors?
Black and white.

What is your favorite bird?
Chicken (delicious).

Fleur Cowles at the entrance to her home in London; the roman brass door knocker was found in 1960 in an antique shop in Rome.

ACKNOWLEDGMENTS

With enormous appreciation and thanks to:

Fleur Cowles, the brightest young thing of all, and Victoria de Rothschild for bringing us together; Nicholas Coleridge for lunch out of the blue; Kim Hersov for her friendship, confidentiality and guidance; Allegra Hicks for her encouragement from the start; Kate Reardon for listening; Rita Konig the patron saint of lost causes; Robert Violette for being so helpful; Karl Lagerfeld; Chanel for getting me the taxi, pronto; Hannah Thomson for giving it a second go; and Stefan, Saffron and Janine for putting up with my endless phone calls; Frank Zachary and Slim Aarons; Graydon Carter; Chiara Bersi Serlini for all of her effort; Robert Higdon; Kip Forbes and Charles, Prince of Wales; Alexandra Kotur; Scott Williams, Starwood Hotels and The Park Lane, Picadilly; and mostly to Robert and Linda Douglass who still know why.

Those who gave of their wits and wisdom: the Countess of Albemarle, Alan Aldridge, Mark Birley, Isabella Blow, Hamish Bowles, Miranda Brooks, Graydon Carter, William Cash, Vassi Chamberlain, Nicholas Coleridge, Fleur Cowles, Amicia de Moubray, Marianne Faithfull, Honor Fraser, Elizabeth Gage, Natasha Garnett, Arthur Hamilton, Nicky Haslam, Rita Konig, Michael Kors, George Lazenby, Michael Lindsay Hogg, Eve McGregor, Donald McLeary, Monica Mason, Lorcan O'Neill, Catherine Ostler, Kate Reardon, Stuart Shave, Paul Smith, HRH Princess Ghida Talal of Jordan, Martyn Thompson, Lucia van der Post, Josh van Gelder, Claus von Bülow, Anita von Pallenberg, Alannah Weston.

Everyone photographed in the book for their trust, patience and support, and, most of all, for their enthusiasm.

Credits: Hannah Thomson, first assistant to Jonathan Becker and production coordinator; Joe Frost of Penny Rich and Cheryl Glover for hair and makeup; L+I Color Lab (E-6), Lali and Inder, and especially Michael Gabor; Sarah Jenkins Lab (black-and-white prints); C-Lab (color processing); Small Darkroom (color prints); i2i (digital color prints).